ABOUT THE AUTHORS

Hilary Maher, BA (Mod.), M.Sc., MBA, is a management consultant working predominantly in Ireland. She is currently employed by the Institute of Public Administration as a specialist in management development and has worked with a wide range of managers in Ireland, Europe and at the United Nations. She has been a manager in the public sector in Ireland and for four years ran a European cultural NGO in Brussels. She has written a wide range of papers on management topics.

Pauline Hall, BA, MA, is a management consultant. Educated in Ireland, France and the US, she has worked as an independent consultant and joined the Institute of Public Administration in 1984 where she helps individuals, teams and organisations across the public sector to manage change. She edited the Network Directory of Women in Management and wrote a textbook on management for the health services. She is also the author of a novel, *Grounds*.

AGENTS OF CHANGE

The Manager's Guide to Planning and Leading Change Projects

Hilary Maher
Pauline Hall

Oak Tree Press
Dublin

Oak Tree Press
Merrion Building
Lower Merrion Street
Dublin 2, Ireland

© 1998 Hilary Maher and Pauline Hall

A catalogue record of this book is
available from the British Library.

ISBN 1 86076 090 2

Printed in the Republic of Ireland
by Colour Books Ltd.

DISCLAIMER

The case studies which are featured in this book are fictional. Any resemblance to any persons or organisations is coincidental. The views in this book are solely those of the authors and do not reflect the work of any other individual or organisation.

ACKNOWLEDGEMENTS

Many people helped us to write this book, including family, friends and colleagues. We would like to thank, in particular, the interviewees who gave generously of their time and experience and whose change stories appear throughout this book.

CONTENTS

Chapter 7

Controlling the Change: Measuring and Monitoring

Chapter 8

Chapter 9

Chapter 10

Introduction

PLANNING AND MANAGING CHANGE

Each time we turn on the news or go into the office, we are faced with change, sometimes momentous, sometimes minor. We are told that change is the new normality and, as we find ourselves approaching the turn of the century, the notion that we are living in a changing world is almost a cliché. Nonetheless, it is borne of real experience, and the fact that it is a cliché does not take away the stress and difficulty that introducing change in the workplace can mean for managers and for their colleagues.

The changes that managers across the public and private sectors find themselves facing today result, in many cases, from such 1990s world-of-work phenomena as:

- "The new economic order", that is, increasing globalisation of industries and sectors and, as a consequence, new influences and distant trends which have to be managed locally

- More regulation of how business is done, such as regulation of workers' rights and health and safety

- Greater use of teamwork in organisations, often coupled with smaller workforces and higher expectations

- The widespread implementation of quality and customer-oriented initiatives as a result of increasing competition and of increasing consumer power, and

- The growing necessity for efficiency and accountability to a wider range of interests and a greater emphasis on ethics in business.

Today's volatile work environment means that only the capacity to change can assure the survival of organisations. Methods which help organisations and leaders to manage these processes of change have become essential, in particular as the changes are happening faster and are becoming more frequent and complex. To illustrate this point, the following is a list of change stories which appeared in *The Irish Times* on 1 January 1998:

- Discussion of the changes which Irish society has undergone over the past 25 years since we joined the EEC/EC/EU

- Plans for the introduction of the Euro on 1 January 1999

- Bookmaker Ladbroke to buy Coral in £375 million deal

- Record flotations of technology companies

- Takeover of New Ireland life assurance company by Bank of Ireland

- Establishment of new IBM plant at Blanchardstown

- Establishment of national register of convicted paedophiles

- IDA sets new targets for job creation in 1998

- Global trading (via the Internet) set to double in the coming year — some retailers' plans to expand their Internet shopping services

- Implementation of a new development package for disadvantaged rural areas

- Plan to halt the spread of "bird flu" in Hong Kong by the slaughter of 1.4 million chickens, ducks and geese in a three-day period.

Much of the change that organisations face these days is driven by external pressures. Nonetheless, even when the driving forces are remote, the change itself is, to some extent, predictable in its impact on organisations and the people who work in them. Thus most changes can be planned and managed. Of course, plans are rarely absolutely perfect, but most managers and most organisations cannot afford not to plan.

This book offers managers a tried-and-tested framework for helping them to manage change in their organisations. The book borrows from project management in several respects, but goes beyond it too. Like project management, it shares the philosophy that change is better planned than unplanned, and that there are tools and techniques which can significantly increase the chances of a plan being as accurate as possible. Unlike much project management, however, this book doesn't require managers to be engineers or "techies" and it puts as much emphasis on the people as it does on the planning. It is, in a sense, "new" project management and, for the sake of simplicity, we use the word "project" in this books to refer to a change.

PROJECT MANAGEMENT — AN EVOLVING DISCIPLINE FOR CHANGING TIMES

If you mention (old) project management, people often think of major initiatives such as the construction of an office block or the computerisation of a payroll system. Nowadays, however, a change project is just as likely to mean the launch of a new product, a programme to prevent accidents or a new customer service initiative.

Project management could probably be traced back to the pyramids, but the modern version most likely began in the middle of this century with the introduction of logistical systems by the US army during World War II. Like the Internet it was born in a highly specialised and technical world and, by the end of the century, has evolved to a stage where it finds a wider public and is applied to all sorts of purposes. Also like the Internet project management has a relatively fixed structure yet this structure can be put to a myriad of uses.

Project management presents organisations and managers with an approach to managing change that helps them to minimise the uncertainty and unpredictability of the changes (projects). Project management provides the basis of a framework for managing change. New project management completes this framework by putting the people side back into perspective and by looking beyond the planning right through to the implementation of the change.

WHAT THIS BOOK IS ABOUT

This book aims to help managers to acquire or extend their change management skills. It offers a fresh look at a subject that is continuing to evolve. It gives equal emphasis to the techniques and to the leadership role within the discipline of change management. It provides a combination of knowledge of the theoretical bases of project management and practical ways in which to use this knowledge in planning and managing change. It is set in a real-life context, with examples of both good and bad practice drawn from current Irish management experience.

This book is for you if:

- You have been just given your first change project to manage

- You have been managing change for some time but would like to tackle future projects more systematically

- You need to acquire or refresh a set of tools and techniques for particular aspects of your change management

- You would like to identify your own strengths and weaknesses by focusing on examples of good and bad performance.

AN OVERVIEW OF THIS BOOK

This is a book of two halves. Part one broadly deals with the theories and techniques of (old) project management as established and as it has grown from its origins in logistics, engineering and, latterly, the IT industry. This part covers such topics as the project environment (locating the customers), planning and scheduling, estimating and budgeting resources and monitoring and controlling their deployment.

Part two deals with the leadership role of the change manager given the reality that if change projects come in on time, to budget, and to the satisfaction of the customer, it is because of the people who made it happen, not the techniques. Equally, if things go wrong, it is people who are the cause and only people who can fix it. Topics covered in this part include leadership style, teamwork, communication, delegation, managing conflict and negotiation.

Chapter 1

A STRUCTURED APPROACH TO MANAGING CHANGE

Welcome to this book on managing change. For those of you who have not already had extensive experience, welcome to change management itself. In joining the ranks of people who are interested in change management, you are joining a vast and diverse group of engineers, information technologists, project managers and general managers who have found a way to help them manage large, complex change programmes.

In this opening chapter, we will set out what we mean by change management in some detail to ensure that we have a common understanding and the beginning of a common terminology with regard to our subject. We will also distinguish the management of change from general management so that we create awareness of the strengths and weaknesses of this structured approach to change management (it is good, but not perfect!).

Finally, we will look at some of the skills required for effective change management. These skills will be developed and consolidated as you progress through this text. Whether you are starting this book as a seasoned manager or as a relative newcomer to managing change, it is recommended that you read all of the case studies to ensure your understanding of the concepts and how they might be applied to change management situations, both real-life and simulated.

THE STRUCTURE OF CHANGE

All change management can be seen (if only with 20:20 hindsight!) to fall into distinct phases. If we use the analogy of a person visiting a doctor, the doctor does not diagnose without an examination of the patient's symptoms and an exploration of how they became ill. The doctor does not decide on a course of action until the diagnosis has been made, and the doctor does not merely prescribe a treatment but also agrees with the patient a follow-up procedure in case of any further problems.

From this analogy, we can deduce the following phases in managing change:

- Exploration of the issue

- Diagnosis of the requirement for change

- Consideration/design of a process or system to bring about that change

- Implementation of the new process or system

- Follow-up to ensure that the process or system has effected the right change.

WHAT IS CHANGE MANAGEMENT?

The best place to start our exploration of change management is to consider the nature or definition of a typical change project.

Change projects usually have some or all of the following features:

- They are concerned with the introduction of something new

- They are often once-off, unique tasks, usually with no exact precedent in the organisation

- These tasks tend to be quite large and "fuzzy" in parts

- They are designed to attain a specific, usually tangible, result

- They require a wide variety of human resources, and

- They are time-limited.

Already these features suggest that change projects are different from other management tasks — they can be more difficult because of the novelty and uncertainty inherent in most changes. They can be harder to manage because they have explicit time limits set for completion and because they usually require a variety of people from different backgrounds, and they often have a higher profile.

Now that we have looked at what a typical change project is, it might be useful to consider what management is. There are hundreds of definitions of management but they all share the basic idea that management is "a purposeful activity entailing the planning, organising and controlling of resources towards the achievement of some pre-defined end(s)". This definition covers all kinds of management, including the management of change.

However, as seasoned managers will quickly tell you, managing change is often very different from other types of management. Given that the above features are typical of change projects, it is perhaps not surprising that many managers find managing change to be so different.

Managing change, then, can be perceived as being more stressful than general management but it is usually seen as being more rewarding than general management too. Table 1.1 gives a summary of the differences identified by many managers and writers between the two types of management.

THE STRENGTHS OF A STRUCTURED APPROACH

So far, we have been looking at the management of change from the perspective of someone who is about to become more closely involved in the process. In order to expand this perspective, we are now going to consider change management in its broader context, that is, as a subset of the activities of a larger organisation. For this reason, we will look at the features of this approach to change management from the point of view of the organisation, from the point of view of its clients, and from the point of view of the change team. This will help you to understand why change management can run into difficulties even in the best organisations regardless of the skills of the manager and his or her team.

Table 1.1: Some Differences between Change Management and General Management

Change Management	General Management
Usually employed for the introduction of unprecedented change	Usually composed of mix of new and routine or repeated tasks
Designed to deliver a single, specific result or goal	"Steady-state" management geared towards the achievement of organisation-wide goals
High degree of control and constraint on a range of performance measures (deadlines, budget, etc.)	No more than usual control and constraint; one performance measure (budget) usually dominant
May involve getting the right people at the right time in the right quantity	Involves managing a group of people (staff) who are there on a more long-term basis
Need to have close regular "user" involvement if change is to succeed	Nice to have "user" involvement if business is to succeed

The Organisation

Change projects form part of the work of organisations (we are using the term "organisation" in a generic sense to include all companies, businesses, offices, etc., whether not-for-profit or private sector). Organisations can benefit from a structured approach to managing change but, for the benefits to accrue, the change must be organised in a certain way:

- Changes are undertaken by a selected group of individuals, of whom most are likely to be employed by one parent organisation

- This group of individuals probably represents a mix of professionals and support staff who are drawn from several parts of the organisation, and

- The changes are seen as part of the overall work of the organisation and, therefore, the goal of the particular change should be seen as consistent with the overall aims and objectives of the organisation.

From this, we can draw the following conclusions:

- Change projects often have to compete for resources (time, people, money, attention, etc.) with other parts of the organisation

- Change teams (or task forces) have a tendency to replicate the structure and working patterns of their parent organisation (for example, if the project is part of the work of a very hierarchical organisation, it is likely that a hierarchy will be the chosen structure for the change team even though hierarchies are not generally the most effective structures for teams), and

- The people involved in the change must see a clear link between it and the overall corporate objectives of the organisation.

The Clients

As we have just seen, changes take place within the context of organisations. Organisations, whether private or public sector, exist to meet the demands and needs of the people who consume their products or services. These consumers can be considered in a number of ways: as simple consumers, as customers, or as clients (to some extent, these terms are used interchangeably in management — the important point is that organisations, including their component parts such as your change team, produce "things" for a specific purpose, i.e. to benefit clients).

Clients, therefore, can also benefit in the following ways from the discipline inherent in this approach to managing change:

- It can give organisations a much greater awareness of their clients (both "internal" and external) through the involvement of "users" (i.e. clients) throughout the change.

- It helps to deliver a result or outcome that is more in accord with what clients need; the impact is, therefore, not only more user-friendly but also usually more sustainable. This is because it gives clients an opportunity to provide a much more considered and detailed specification of the nature and type of result(s) which they require from the change.

These client benefits rarely happen by chance, however. Good relationships with clients must be actively managed and often must be preceded by education about the change. Such education is often necessary so that these clients can assert themselves in the world of professional managers and so that they can accurately specify the result they want — as we shall see later, both the clients and also the change manager (and team) who suffer if the wrong result is delivered, even if this wrong result was due to poor specification by the client.

The Change Team

Just as this structured approach to managing change can benefit organisations and clients, so too can it be rewarding for the change project personnel (you and your team members). You may have already identified a number of these benefits, such as:

- Regular progress reporting and feedback, which are typical of this type of change management, can also be hugely motivating for staff

- Team members get much greater opportunities for multi-skilling than do staff in typical line management

- There is often a certain elitism involved in being asked to be a member of a particular change team

- Change team members are more likely to be dedicated (i.e. work only on the change) and protected from interference than staff in line management.

SOME CHANGE MANAGEMENT SKILLS

Each of the phases of any change project involves a variety of skills, most of which are the skills of good general management and have probably already been acquired to some extent by you and your team. Structuring change helps to ensure that the right skills are used by the right people at the right time.

Some of the key management skills in relation to the different phases of a change project are shown in Table 1.2.

Table 1.2: Key Change Management Skills

Exploration	Communication skills, such as interviewing, probing, re-framing, listening, questioning, summarising, analysing, etc.
Diagnosis	Decision-making and problem-solving
Design	Team-building, communication, conflict resolution, estimating, planning
Implementation	Negotiation, conflict resolution, teamwork, delegation, communication, motivating, influencing, etc.
Follow-Up	Monitoring, controlling, reviewing and communicating.

These are the principal skills involved in successfully managing change. In addition, the success of your change management can be almost guaranteed if the following also apply:

- Support from top management or, at least, from a top manager who can "champion the cause" should problems occur

- Adequate resources (time, people and money in the right combinations)

- A strong awareness of the client or end-user of the intended result of the change

- A clear definition of the roles and responsibilities within the team and of the organisation and the client

- An element of flexibility — things can alter during the life of the change project, both within the project and in the outside world and the manager and team often have no option but to change too, and

- Luck — it always helps but it's rarely enough on its own!

Many of the issues introduced in this chapter will be dealt with in much greater detail in later chapters. Our goal will be to help you to diagnose any problems in your management of change and to then move towards designing and implementing workable solutions to them.

Chapter 2

THE ENVIRONMENT OF THE CHANGE

Chapter 1 opened up the topic of change management, and especially the fact that change arises in specific circumstances. Your past experience may have illustrated how the "pure" theory of managing change often needs to be practised in a very "impure" environment.

No change project occurs in a vacuum. When you are first given responsibility for managing one, you might begin by posing a few questions. Why this project, why now, why here, and why with this particular aim? This chapter is designed to help you to see the change you are to manage in its larger context — the big picture.

All triggers for change arise within the larger environment, known as the *macro environment*. Developments in the current political, cultural, economic, legal, technological and sociological areas affect the operations of your organisation as a whole, including the part to which you belong. Such factors are known, collectively, as PESTER factors. This acronym stands for **P**olitical, **E**conomic, **S**ocial, **T**echnological, **E**cological and **R**egulatory (including Legal). For you, most of these factors are already given: they influence the genesis of your change project. However, they are not easily influenced by you.

The PESTER factors are important to anyone who is managing a change. However, of even more significance to you is the more immediate environment of your change, the *task environment*. The task environment is critical because it includes all potential collaborators, competitors and "clients" of your change. This task environment can directly influence you (just like the macro environment) but what makes the task environment more significant is that the influence can go *both* ways, i.e. you can have much more influence over it than you can over the macro environment.

STAKEHOLDERS AND CHANGE

The effect of environmental influences on change projects is often to limit the choices available to the change manager. Frequently, managers have to take the definition of the change as given, and concentrate on the scope for decision-making that they have available to them in reality. This is chiefly at the level of implementation. Accurate reading of the environment of the change will optimise the room to manoeuvre. This reading of the environment is not an exercise in philosophical speculation but rather in managerial "know-how", and is as vital as the technical and professional knowledge which led to you being chosen to lead the change in the first place.

To manage your environment effectively, you need to start by identifying the stakeholders and then work out how best to relate to them. They are affected by, and can affect, the change for which you have responsibility. Very simply, "stakeholders" are individuals, groups or organisations that have an interest or a stake in the outcome of a project.

A commonly used technique for considering where stakeholders might lie in relation to any proposed issue is called a *force field analysis*. This technique comes from the world of physics and can be a powerful way of assessing one's strength and anticipating resistance in relation to any change project. The technique is based on mapping or diagramming.

Figure 2.1 shows simply that, for any situation to remain in its status quo (i.e. unchanged), there must be an equal amount of energy spent in wanting to change it ("propellers") and in wanting to keep it the same ("resistors").

It follows, then, that for change to occur, the stasis must be disturbed. This can only be achieved by changing the balance of the forces, i.e. by removing one or more of the resisting forces, by adding one or more propelling forces, or by doing both.

Figure 2.1: Force Field Analysis

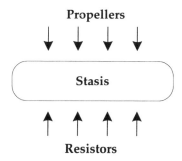

A simple example of how this might look in a "real" change situation is shown below in Figure 2.2 in relation to the problem of changing workers' attitudes to compliance with mandatory health and safety regulations (specimen only — not intended to represent full picture of reality).

Figure 2.2: Sample Force Field Analysis

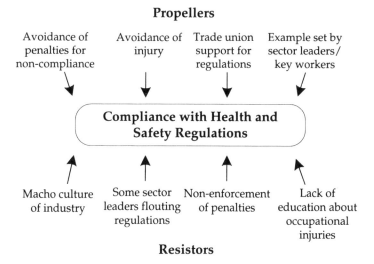

If you were to do a quick-and-dirty force field analysis for the change that you are managing, you will probably identify a large number of different propelling and resisting forces in your diagram. Some of these forces will be internally-based and some will be external. Internally-based forces are, in general, closer to you in their goals and aspirations and often more amenable to influence than are external forces. For example, in Figure 2.2 the internal forces are those that relate to the culture and values of the organisation (key stakeholders here would be the staff themselves and senior management) and the external forces are those that are related to the industry as a whole. If we were doing a force field diagram for a change project on staff appraisal schemes, we might find that more of the forces were internal (to the organisation and its structure and culture) than external (international trends towards more comprehensive performance measurement).

The reason it is useful to make the distinction between the internal and external forces is because, in general, we can have more immediate influence and control over the internal forces (the external forces are often PESTER environmental factors). Thus, in prioritising which of the forces we should work on first, it usually makes sense to start on the internal ones (propellers or resistors).

ANALYSING STAKEHOLDERS

In addition to a force field analysis, the following questions should help you to identify the stakeholders in your change:

- Who has expressed or is expressing a need for this change?

- Who is taking a lead in promoting this change?

- Who has relevant responsibility, power and status to "make or break" this change?

- Who will participate in the change planning and implementation?

- Who shapes or influences opinion about the issues?

- Which demographic (or other) groups are affected by the situation?

- Who has a role with regard to the situation? Is everybody's role clear to us and to them?

Now begin to analyse how significant each stakeholder is. Ask yourself: how likely are they to impact on the success of your change project? What is the direction of their influence (supportive or competitive/subversive)? How strong is their influence?

In establishing the position of your stakeholders, the most important factor is the likelihood of their having an impact on you and on your change project. However, the best approach is to answer questions about the strength and direction first, and then consider the likelihood.

The matrix shown in Figure 2.3 will help you here. Use it to locate each stakeholder in terms of the strength and direction of their potential influence on you. When this is done, allocate a rating (between 1 and 5) to each stakeholder in terms of the likelihood of their influence on you.

Figure 2.3: Mapping Stakeholder Interests

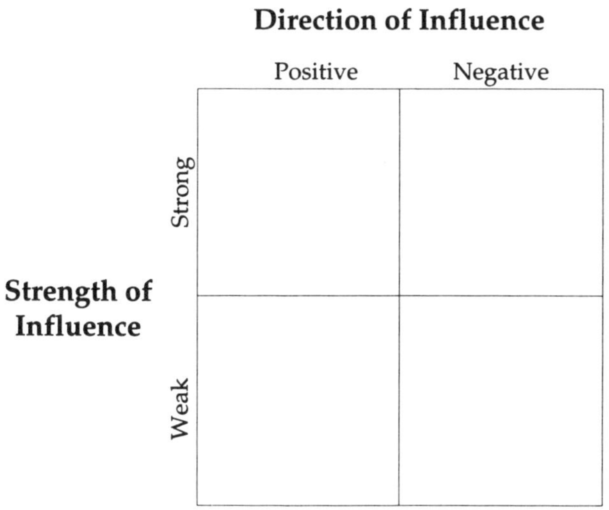

Direction of Influence

	Positive	Negative
Strong		
Weak		

Strength of Influence

Stakeholders can affect you, whether you are aware of their influence or not. If you know your stakeholders and their interests, you can begin to anticipate their behaviour and adjust your own behaviour accordingly. Any stakeholder you rated as being likely to have a strong influence will need careful managing. You will need to check out how much you know about them. If you don't know whose influence is strong, or whether it is positive or negative, you need to make some assumptions and, importantly, check out the validity behind your assumptions. Also, remember that the strength and direction of a stakeholder's influence can vary during the life of your change project.

You will be most concerned with those who have a potentially high impact (negative or positive) and are also likely to affect the situation.

Now you need to "get inside the head" of some of your most powerful stakeholders. This involves putting yourself in their position, thinking about what is important to them, what their goals and objectives are, what their fears and concerns are. By doing this, it will become clear to you where any clash of interests between you might lie. Focus in particular on those stakeholders whom you rated as having a strong potential influence on you.

After doing this exercise, you should be able to refine your list of stakeholders, by identifying those about whom you lack knowledge and/or whose objectives are likely to coincide or compete with yours.

This will help you to focus on gathering the information that is lacking, since you cannot manage what you are not aware of. Also, it can be very instructive to check to what extent you have thought through your own stance.

MANAGING STAKEHOLDER RELATIONSHIPS

Managers have a number of options available to them as to how best to manage relationships with stakeholders. As a change manager, you need, first of all, to decide what you are aiming to achieve in your relationship with each stakeholder. Put very crudely, do you want a *colder* relationship with them (greater *autonomy* from them) or do you want a *warmer* relationship with them (more *in common* between the two of you)? The various options can be seen in Figure 2.4 below.

Figure 2.4: Managing Stakeholders Continuum

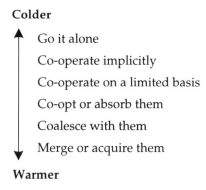

Colder

Go it alone

Co-operate implicitly

Co-operate on a limited basis

Co-opt or absorb them

Coalesce with them

Merge or acquire them

Warmer

If you are aiming to minimise your dependence on stakeholders, you will work as far as possible at the top of this continuum. This can mean *"going it alone"*, i.e. pursuing your own agenda and seeking to publicise and win support for that agenda or *implicitly co-operating* with the other party.

If, on the other hand, your stakeholders have so much power that your room to manoeuvre is limited, you have to find a degree of commonality with them, however costly that is to you in terms of your autonomy. Thus, you might agree to *co-operate* for a limited time or in relation to a limited area of work or you might decide that the best way of managing them is to invite one of their representatives on to your change management team (*co-option*).

The third way of looking at the relationship is interdependence (*coalition* or *merger*). Here, you acknowledge that you cannot be independent of a particular stakeholder, and you both explicitly agree to join forces because there are mutual benefits, for example, in greater security and certainty about your task environments.

The whole issue of working with stakeholders comes to life when you begin to plan the activities of your change and to identify its different stages. Generally, you will find most difficulty where your achievement of a deadline depends on someone else completing it or where events can progress only when someone else has completed a separate activity (dependent activity).

Case Study

Anna Ryan was the director of a social services organisation which had received a large grant from Europe to launch and run a local employment and entrepreneurial development programme. When she took on the job she thought it looked fairly straightforward — it was a question of providing seed capital and technical support to potential new small business start-ups. The criteria for eligibility were quite broad and preliminary research had shown that the area was well-endowed with skilled professionals, crafts people, and people commuting to Dublin who were looking for ways to work closer to home. Her job then, as she saw it, was to match up these people with the programme.

However, as news and publicity about the programme spread, it became clear that not everybody saw the programme as good news and that there were people who were concerned about its implications for the area. For example, people who were already in business in the area were less than happy because they had had to finance their own businesses, yet this programme would provide the same seed capital to potential competitors. In addition, some of the state agencies were displeased because the criteria for support under this scheme were at odds with those of the more established state business development schemes, and some of the banks didn't like the fact that they might lose out on potential new borrowers. Finally, as the programme got underway, it ran into problems when the local media gave widespread coverage to two well-connected applicants whose applications were turned down for support (they were looking for grants to adapt their homes for their businesses but this fell outside the scope of the scheme).

So, as time went on, it became clear to Anna that she would have to spend time building relationships with potential clients of the programme but, more significantly, she would also have to spend a good deal more time than she had bargained for with a lot of other people as well if the programme was going to work. Her "strategy" for dealing with the various stakeholders was as follows:

Strong Influence	
Potential Applicants: Get as close as possible to them	Disseminate information about the programme to as many as possible and, in particular, to target groups most likely to apply and meet the eligibility criteria (such as commuters, skilled trades people, etc.)
Media/Local Radio: Aim for "warm" relations	Get to know them and secure publicity for the programme — provide them with regular "good news" stories about local people who were benefiting from the programme.
Public Representatives: Aim for "warm" relations	Give them full details on the programme, meet them and explain the programme and its criteria to them. Keep them posted on progress, especially about people in their localities.
Banks: Try to make things less competitive, less "cold"	Meet with local bank managers, explain the programme to them. Tell them about type of applicants, i.e. people who would not normally get bank loans for new businesses and who might be looking to the banks for future loans if their businesses succeed.
Weak Influence	
Other Statutory Agencies: Aim for less "cold" relations	Meet with them to explain the programme in full to them and to explain criteria for eligibility and application process. Look for areas where the different schemes might complement each other.
Established Businesses in the Area: "Warm" them up for the future	Try to get the support of established businesses in the area so that, at a future stage, a "buddy" system can be set up between new entrepreneurs and established local business managers.
European Union/ Directorate General V	Keep Brussels informed of progress. Don't antagonise them by submitting necessary reports late or incomplete.

Chapter 3

IDENTIFYING AND INITIATING THE CHANGE

INTRODUCTION

In Chapter 1, we saw how and why the management of change is different from the routine work of an organisation or manager. We saw that change projects are often "once-offs", i.e. specific, time-limited, goal-oriented pieces of work. We also saw that they need to be actively managed from beginning to end, in both their big picture context and in their detail.

In this chapter, we will focus on the beginning or start-up phase of change projects. Because change management is goal-oriented, there is a strong requirement that the *right* goal be identified and agreed at the earliest stage. Unfortunately, newspapers, management textbooks and even specialist journals contain plenty of stories about changes which were executed perfectly but which delivered the wrong goal — they were efficient, but not effective. Examples which spring to mind are the launch of products which met no market (such as the ill-fated Guinness Light) and the introduction of "solutions" to social problems which either lie dormant or cause worse problems (e.g. adding extra road capacity instead of looking at other transport options). In such cases, the products are often perfectly delivered but the wrong demand, or the wrong way of meeting a demand, was identified.

How can people be so irrational, you are probably asking? It is easy. For example, imagine you want to build a house for yourself and you commission an architect to draw up the plans. You give the architect quite a detailed specification of the house you want:

you want it to have two bathrooms, four bedrooms, face south-west, have a large open living area downstairs to allow for both dining and recreation and a small room, also downstairs, which is to serve as an office. The house must be at least two metres back from the street and, you add, you have no more than £150,000 to spend on the building of the house (including the architect's fees, materials, etc.). How many options for the design of the house within these specifications do you think an architect might be able to imagine? How would you feel if, at the end of six months, the architect presented you with a house which met your technical specification but you found that your family didn't like it at all — it was too dark, the bedrooms were too small, there was no garden and the kitchen was not at all "user-friendly"? Or worse, you found that nobody had checked the local authority's plans for the area and, five years later, you find that a four-lane ring-road is to be built twenty metres from your front garden. . . .

In this example, it is easy to imagine that you would be in close contact with the architect throughout the development of the house and so you would be able to monitor the house at each stage and, therefore, prevent him building a house that didn't meet your needs. And, of course, you'd check the plans for the vicinity before buying the plot of land, wouldn't you?

In reality, organisational change projects are often managed with much less consultation during their lifecycle, which makes getting a full and accurate specification at the start even more important. In addition, "real-life" changes are often designed to deliver results which are much less tangible than a house — they might be designed to put a new health programme in place or to deliver a new leisure product to meet the opportunities presented by the "grey pound". Changes such as these need a great deal of discussion and definition at the beginning so that the change team delivers the result that the client actually wants.

DEFINING THE SCOPE OF A CHANGE

The scope of a change refers to its size. How big a change are you being asked to take on? Are you to undertake all aspects of the change or are there other agencies or groups of people undertaking bits of it as well?

The role of the manager in defining the scope of a change is to try to identify where are the boundaries of the change itself and what are the limits of the responsibilities of the team in relation to it. This definition cannot be done by the manager alone. The input of the client is also critical here.

It is useful to draw a distinction here between different types of client. It is quite possible that there will be a "commissioning client" who is quite separate from the end-user ("end client") of the change. For example, in new product launches, the commissioning client is often to be found within the company — the Board of Directors or Managing Director, acting on behalf of shareholders, may have commissioned the new product. However, the end clients are those who will actually buy and use the product. The needs of these two types of clients, in relation to the same change, will be very different.

If you, as the manager of the change, have access only to the commissioning clients, there is an element of risk inherent in your definition of the scope of the project.

AGREEING THE OBJECTIVES OF THE CHANGE

Defining the goal of the change is, as we have said, critical to effective change management. It is important to try to spend a bit of time at this stage with clients (both types, if possible) so as to ensure that you have an agreed definition of the purpose of the change. As a preliminary to setting out a statement of the objectives of the change, these are the main questions you need to have answered:

- What difference is this change supposed to make to the lives of the clients? What improvement will this change make to the lives of the end clients? What would be their criteria for success in relation to this change?

- What problem will be solved by this change? Will any others be caused?

- What gap or opportunity will this change meet?

- How does this goal relate to the goals of the organisation and to other goals of the commissioning client?

Quite often, these questions take time to answer. The clients may be unclear about what they want, or they may be unwilling to specify exactly what they want because the change is too sensitive or because they might fail to achieve what they want. In addition, the clients may be unwilling to commit themselves to achieving a specific result.

Notwithstanding these difficulties, it is worth the effort to stay at this stage until each party is clear about what they want the change to achieve. This is one of the major opportunities for you, as manager of this change, to manage the expectations of the clients and it is worth remembering here that "the less people know for sure, the more they tend to expect". The use of a variety of tools and methods can help all parties to reach clarity about what they want from the change (e.g. tools and methods such as concept simulation, models, mock-ups, scenarios, visualisation, pictures, stories, etc.).

The answers to these questions will provide a great deal of "soft" (qualitative) information about the change. However, as a manager you are also interested in the "harder" (quantifiable) information, such as how much time you have available, how will the change be resourced, etc. All too often, change management is typified by a great deal of clarity about the "hard" factors (the commissioning client will only supply a budget of £xxx,xxx and wants the goal reached as early as possible) and very little clarity about the "soft" side. Your job is to make sure that you are as clear as you can be about both the hard and the soft aspects so that neither gets lost in the inevitable drive to get it finished. A useful way of ensuring there is clarity about both sides is to think of a change as having three dimensions, each of which must be clear before the project can begin, as illustrated in Figure 3.1.

Figure 3.1: The Three Aspects of Change Objectives

Quality

Time   **Cost**

This diagram shows that a change has three aspects, two hard (time and cost — "hard" because they are quantifiable and measurable) and one soft (quality — "soft" because it is usually difficult to define or measure with precision). Given this imbalance between hard and soft, the aspect which you must devote most energy to defining is quality; otherwise you will probably evaluate progress only in terms of adherence to schedule and to budgets.

In essence, the three questions here for you are:

- How *much* (money do we have)?

- How *long* (in terms of time do we have)?

- How *good* (how strong must the impact of this change be or how great a difference does it have to make?)?

In practice, what often happens is that the commissioning client sets a limit on the amount of money to be spent, the commissioning client and end client want the change to be in place as soon as possible, and everyone wants to achieve the "best ever" result.

Thus, not only is the potential for conflict built into the change but you may be left to find a balance between the three aspects.

The strong messages for managers in setting the objectives of any change are, therefore, as follows:

1. The job of the manager could be described as that of a balancing mechanism since an alteration in any aspect of the change will have implications for one or both of the other two. For example, if something happens which causes the change to take more time than planned, this will have an impact on the budget. If both the budget and the time available are absolutely fixed, any variation from the plan is likely to compromise the quality of the result. If the budget is cut back, either the project will take longer to complete or the quality will have to be reduced.

2. It is virtually impossible to manage a change which is fixed in terms of time, cost *and* quality — in practice, something always happens to force alterations in one or more of these aspects during the life of the change. Managers should try to protect themselves by asking the commissioning clients to give their opinion on which of the three aspects is/are (a) most likely to vary from the plan and (b) what steps they would like taken in relation to one or both of the other two variables should unplanned variation(s) occur.

3. A critical skill for change managers, given that variations almost always occur (life is never exactly as we plan it), is negotiation, as it is only by negotiation that you will be able to achieve ongoing balance between the three aspects of the change objectives.

THE TERMS OF REFERENCE OF THE CHANGE

Having reached agreement on the scope and objectives of the change, you are now at the stage where you can consider committing yourself and your client to paper. A document summarising the size and scope of the required change is often referred to as the *Terms of Reference*. Briefly, this document is useful because it summarises the agreements reached to date with the clients, and serves as a briefing document for everyone else who is interested. A common way of drafting Terms of Reference is shown in Table 3.1 below.

Table 3.1: Contents of Terms of Reference Document

Background	A brief description of the origins of the problem or situation which requires the change. Details of any similar work done in the past in the same area. Details of the main agencies and clients involved.
Goal/Purpose	A statement of the agreed purpose of the change describing the impact or outcome that is required.
Scope	A summary of the size of the change and of the team's involvement at different stages.
Time/Cost	Estimates of the budget and of the time which the change will require.
Quality	An indication of the standard which the change is required to meet and some idea of how this standard will be measured.
Outline Plan	An outline of the main phases of the project and the output of each phase.

ASSESSING THE STRATEGIC RISK OF A CHANGE

As discussed in Chapter 1, all change projects are inherently risky. There is risk associated with planning, risk associated with implementation and risk associated with each of the aspects of change management discussed in this chapter, namely, defining the scope and setting the objectives of the change. You cannot remove all of the risk from projects but you do need to be aware of the risk that is entailed at each stage.

A rough "rule of thumb" about the risk associated with change management is that the further you are from implementation, the more risk is involved. Thus, the early stages of the change management, i.e. the stages covered in this chapter, are potentially the most risky stages. The risk associated with defining scope and setting objectives is *strategic* risk — strategic because its implications for the rest of the change can be enormous.

Part of your role is to monitor and analyse risk during a change project. This risk assessment starts here. At this early stage, risk assessment includes a review of the overall *feasibility* of the change.

The assessment of strategic risk seeks to identify the major uncertainties and assumptions that may affect the change and its environment. Significant assumptions which may be risky, for example, would be that nothing about the environment will alter during the life of the change, that the goal will be just as desirable at the end as it was at the start, that there is only "one right way" of achieving the goal, etc. Areas of uncertainty about the feasibility include, for example, whether the gains will be sustainable when the change has happened, whether the organisation has the know-how and culture to facilitate the change, whether there is a genuine need for *this* change (rather than some other one), etc.

You cannot know the answers to all of these questions and so it is recommended that you consult with key individuals at this stage about the overall feasibility and level of agreement about the change. Even if these questions cannot be answered with certainty following this type of consultation, by consulting with others you will have at least spread some of the risk involved by making clear to key individuals any concerns about the risk and/or feasibility of the change at this stage.

Here is a quick checklist which may help you to identify any risky assumptions that you or others might be making about the change:

1. What could change during the life of this change project (within the team and the organisation or in the environment)?

2. How will I know if I still have agreement between the key parties involved with the project?

3. What assumptions am I making about our own competence?

4. What assumptions am I making about the benefits of the change?

5. What is telling me (or others) that the project is feasible?

6. Is there another (perhaps simpler) way of achieving the same outcome?

Extract from Interview — *Project Manager, Financial Services Company*

"Tell us a bit about the change, about what it was that you were introducing."

"OK, well, the product was a new life assurance and pensions product. The company already had a very simple life assurance product but the new product was a much more sophisticated, more modern life assurance policy. It was, effectively, a UK product that was being slotted into the Irish company. The main idea was to build on the market share which the company had already established through its other life assurance, accident and health care products. It was envisaged that it would have relatively wide appeal but, initially, the focus was on the existing client segment of the market.

When I was brought in to the company [to manage this project], I was told that my job was to set up the full range of administrative systems which would be required to back up the product. The main thing was get the systems up and running in time for the launch date. The launch date was set for nine months out so we had nine months to set up pretty complex processing and IT systems, get the documentation and backup literature ready, get the licensing seen to, do all of the necessary preparatory work."

"In the launch of any change, and in the management of it, there are three aspects to it (quality, time and cost). You mentioned the timing. In

relation to the cost, is it fair to say that the costs were a given by the time you came on board?"

"Yeah, the budget was set in the sense that they knew how much they had to get the product to the market by then. The overall budget ceiling was controlled by the UK parent. I had control over all of the operational aspects of the budget, such as staffing, some of the promotional costs, systems set-up, recruitment, etc. I had control over how the money was spent, such as how many staff, who to recruit, and so on. I also had a contingency in case of major unforeseen costs arising but I didn't want to have to touch that – it might have looked like sloppy planning or control and I was just new in to this company."

"Was the nine-month deadline that you were given absolute, non-negotiable?"

"I took it to be, I never even considered not meeting that deadline, it just wasn't an issue. It was fixed and I got agreement from senior management that everything else, all other 'routine' work, was secondary to meeting this deadline. Also, I knew from my experience in other companies that this deadline should have given us more than enough time — I had set up similar systems in less."

"And what about the quality — how did you know when you had achieved what you set out to achieve?"

"Well, we had sales targets and client satisfaction targets, as well as our own internal control targets. In the nature of things, you get the information back to you first about sales performance so, early on, this becomes the most critical aspect of quality.

In fact, the product hugely exceeded the sales target that had been set for the first two years — we could see after 18 months that the target had been set too low because sales were much higher than we ever anticipated, but the reasons for that became quite clear when, suddenly, after about two years, business started falling off . . . it transpired that it was a question of quantity, not quality. The customers weren't complaining, they just weren't buying any more and our quality control systems weren't good enough to tell us why. Also, believe it or not, the sales force didn't have any quality targets set for them — sell as many as you can was the idea and there was very poor control over the methods and the reward system was badly designed. They got paid up front for signing up business so, if business lapsed or was cancelled after a year or so, we found it very difficult to recoup any money from the sales people. Many of them in fact left after a year or so: they made the easy sales, made a lot of money, then left knowing that the business would not stand long term.

So, to cut a long story short, the product succeeded in terms of quantity of business but the nature of the life assurance business is all your costs are met up front and a product needs to stay on your books for seven or eight years before anybody starts to make money on it. So, at the end of the day, the product cost the company about £3 million net and, in fact, the Irish end of that business was closed down a few years later. The company paid the price for being sales-driven rather than market-driven. I suppose you could say that it won the battle but lost the war."

"It seems pretty unbelievable that a company could fail to notice what was happening and end up losing this amount of money — in hindsight, why or how do you think this happened?"

"Well, yes, I suppose it is hard to believe. . . . Fortunately, I had moved on by the time this happened so I don't know whether they did their own evaluation of the whole episode or, if they did, what they found out. In my opinion, lots of things contributed to it — first of all, the company's strength was its selling focus and it thought this would apply in any market — it specialised in low-profit, high-volume products, pretty much like a supermarket. But the life assurance market is a very lucrative one and companies were coming in all the time and those who were winning were the ones who were competing on the basis of very flexible user-friendly policies and good customer support, customised policies rather than the commodity-type one which we were selling.

There were internal problems too, well, problems might be too strong a word, but, for instance, I was the project manager yet the sales force didn't come within my control so it was quite late into the project by the time that we realised that the sales force was concentrating on selling lots of policies rather than selling a smaller number to customers who were likely to hold on to them. When this problem became evident, there was a kind of power struggle because it was becoming obvious that some people wanted to focus on high volume and others wanted to focus on better sales but nobody really wanted to confront this issue and, by the time senior management in the UK were brought in, the damage had been done.

So, from my point of view, the company culture was a major contributory factor — its selling focus and, because selling was considered so sacrosanct, nobody wanted to challenge the sales department — it was like questioning God to question the sales tactics."

Chapter 4

PLANNING THE CHANGE: STRUCTURING

INTRODUCTION

Plans are, in essence, controlled predictions about the future. They are attempts to approximate reality as we think it will happen. Most of us are familiar with the cliché of plans that sit on shelves in offices. In change planning, the real test of a plan is in its implementation, not its construction. Plans are not infallible and are rarely wholly accurate. If a plan is to have any chance of being an accurate guide to the future, it must be "live", that is, a working document which is revised and rewritten to take account of circumstances as they unfold, rather than a series of predictions which are "written in stone". Plans in change management are a means to an end, not an end in themselves.

There is no doubt that change planning can be time-consuming and arduous, especially to people who prefer to think "about the whole rather than the pieces". One of the best ways of making planning more interesting and of improving the plan is to involve other people in drawing it up. If you already know who you will be working with on the change, involve them. Involving the clients, either representatives of the commissioning clients or of the end clients, also can have great "bullet-proofing" benefits.

Change planning consists of two types of activity: structuring the work and scheduling the work. Structuring involves identifying *what* needs to be done and scheduling involves identifying *when* it needs to be done. Experience suggests that it is best to separate the two activities. Chapter 5 deals with Scheduling.

Case Study

Gerry has recently been appointed to manage the "City Means Business" change project.

"I can't believe I'm hearing this. You're seriously telling me that we've ended up with two databases", Gerry groaned. Only the day before, he was congratulating himself on how he had prepared a comprehensive plan for the project on Inner-City Renewal he was managing. The first phase of the change project was entitled Data Collection. This was supposed to deliver an accurate and up-to-date profile of the area's potential for the location of enterprises.

Gerry discovered that both the Community Association and the Local Authority had separately drawn up registers of vacant business premises. As he planned it, there would be one database available for access by any number of organisations. When he called them, the Local Authority and the Community Association defended their decision. It occurred to Gerry that here were two groups working very hard on producing the same material and, worse, he couldn't offend either.

His colleague, Mary, suggested that it might be worth checking if the two databases were in any way complementary. Gerry found that, whilst there was considerable overlap, the Community Association register concentrated more on service companies and the Local Authority one on manufacturing. He saw, therefore, some scope to use the duplication of effort in a positive way.

He met both groups of representatives together and pointed out what had happened. He secured their agreement to avoid further haphazard repetition. For him, this meant negotiating a role that included more explicit and active management of the collaboration process. For them, it entailed the addition of new tasks (e.g. consultation with Gerry before they undertook initiatives) and new activities (e.g. analysis of gaps and overlaps) in their work on later phases. Though the setback caused delay, it led to the production of a high-quality deliverable: a very user-friendly consolidated database. It would, however, have been in all their interests if he had started by involving them in preparing his plan.

CREATING A WORK BREAKDOWN STRUCTURE

A Work Breakdown Structure (WBS) is a way of organising the work of change projects according to a consistent and logical analysis of the components of the change. It breaks down a change project into "chunks" of work which themselves can be broken down into smaller chunks. This chunking serves two purposes:

1. It ensures all the work is planned (without gaps or overlaps), and

2. It helps to ensure that responsibility for each chunk of work has been allocated to some individual (or group).

Below is a simplified and generic Work Breakdown Structure. This WBS fits a large number of changes and is often a good place to start your own change breakdown. Change itself can be broken down into a number of predictable phases (as we saw in Chapter 1). This can be depicted in a diagram format as shown in Figure 4.1.

Figure 4.1: Standard or Generic Work Breakdown Structure

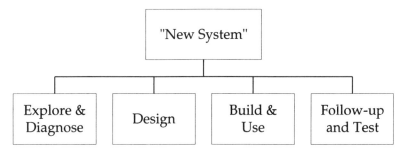

Of course, this is just the start of breaking down the work of introducing a new system. This generic WBS is a "one-size-fits-all" version, which can serve as the skeleton for structuring any change.

One of the most useful techniques for identifying the major phases of a WBS is to brainstorm with a number of people. Brainstorming works best when ideas are thrown (without evaluation or any attempt to order them) onto an area visible to all members of the group. (If a whiteboard is not available, use "post-it" notes on a wall.) After the "stock" of ideas has been exhausted, these ideas can be organised into chunks or related "superchunks". You can, of course, do this on your own but you are less likely to overlook some key "chunk" if there are other people, in addition to you, thinking about it. This may sound obvious, but overlooking components of the change is one of the most frequent faults in change plans.

Levels of Planning

When does a chunk become a superchunk? To some extent, there is no absolute or clear-cut answer to this question as it is usually relative to the complexity of the change. What constitutes a level in one change project may well differ from a level in another project. There are some general rules, however, about how to break down work into consistent levels (i.e. consistent in terms of their size and/or importance). In planning conventions, lower levels are usually indented for the sake of ease of use, as shown in Figure 4.2.

Figure 4.2: Levels of Planning

Change Master Plan
Phase Plans
Tasks
Subtasks
Activities

The Change Master Plan is the plan for the entire change project, from exploration/feasibility through to implementation and follow-up. The Phase Plans are the plans for each of the major phases, consisting of all of the pieces of work that are necessary to complete each phase. The pieces of work are organised into Tasks, which are pieces of work with an identifiable start and finish and whose completion can be measured. Tasks are frequently delegated to team members so the task should be understandable as a whole piece of work. Depending on the complexity of the individual tasks, they are broken down into Subtasks and Activities or just to Activities. In general, Activities are pieces of work of no more than about 35 hours of effort.

In Chapter 2 the house-building example was introduced to illustrate how objectives are set. We can continue with this example to demonstrate how this house-building project might break down into the different planning levels we have been discussing.

Figure 4.3: Sample WBS for New House Project

Change Project

Build New House

Phases

1.0 Client Specification
2.0 Design
3.0 Construction
4.0 Fitting/Decorating

Tasks (for Phase 2.0)

2.1 *Check blueprint library for best fit to specification*
2.2 *Computer modifications to best match exact specification*
2.3 *Costings using different materials*
2.4 *Client test*
2.5 *Client approval*

Subtasks (for Task 2.2)

2.2.1 *Check blueprint for degree of fit*
2.2.2 *Major modification to match best fit to exact client specification*
2.2.3 *Materials modification options*

Activities (for Subtask 2.2.3)

2.2.3.1 *Produce low cost materials option*

2.2.3.2 *Produce high cost materials option*

2.2.3.3 *Produce most durable materials option*

This example of a WBS is incomplete, of course, in that it only shows elements of the Task/Subtask/Activity levels for one of the four phases of building the house. To complete the WBS, you would have to detail these levels for the other three phases too. The final WBS should represent a pyramid and the width at the base of this pyramid will reflect the number of phases and their tasks/subtasks, which in turn will reflect the complexity of the project in question.

In summary, here are a few guidelines which should help in creating a Work Breakdown Structure for any change:

- There is no one right way of organising the breakdown: it can be by function or discipline, by component, by nature of work, etc.

- Remember that each level should be a more detailed expansion of the level immediately above it

- The degree of detail should be fairly consistent for each level

- The subdivision of work should always continue down to the task level as, in general, responsibility is easiest to assign at this level and it is at this level that gaps or overlaps usually become apparent, and

- Finally, remember that it is much simpler if you do not attempt to sequence the work at this stage.

TESTING THE PLAN USING INPUTS AND DELIVERABLES

We said earlier in this chapter that one of the reasons why you would bother to plan your change project is so that you can ensure that you have allocated (or taken) responsibility for all of the work of the change and that there are no gaps or overlaps.

One of the ways of making sure this happens is to identify the linkages between the different tasks. This is done by checking that the required *inputs* for each task are secured or available and that the required *deliverable(s)* from each task have been identified. Inputs and deliverables refer, respectively, to what goes into doing a task (e.g. resources, such as people, information, ideas, materials, etc.) and what comes out of doing that task (e.g. tangible products, such as reports, models, drafts, etc.). Every part of a change project has a certain number of inputs and a certain number of deliverables which, in general, feed forward into each other — in other words, inputs are processed to make deliverables which either themselves become inputs for the next or later stage(s) in the work chain or which can stand alone (e.g. progress reports to clients).

In the house-building example, the phase titles themselves (as is often the case) give a good indication of the deliverables expected from each. From *Client Specification*, we would expect a specification for the house that was agreed between the client and the architect; from *Design*, we would expect an architect-produced design that was approved by the client to their exact cost and quality specification; from *Construction*, we would expect a built house and, from *Fitting/Decorating*, we would expect a house which was ready for occupation.

A rough check between the four phases tells us that, in this case, the deliverable from the first phase (i.e. the agreed specification) is a necessary input to the second phase, the deliverable from the second phase (i.e. the agreed design) is a necessary input to the third phase, and so on. This logical chain of inputs → deliverables → inputs across the phases shows us that we are unlikely to have omitted any phase and that our plan is internally consistent.

If, for example, it was found that a deliverable was "left over" (that is, it did not relate to a further phase or had no value in itself) the next question would have to be: "why is it being delivered?" Equally, if we found that an input into a certain phase was required but that input had not been budgeted (another common occurrence in change management!), the plan would need to be double-checked.

The same model is used at the next level down, that is, at the Task and Activity levels. In relation to each task or activity, the inputs and the deliverables need to be identified. This, again, will allow you to check that critical tasks have not been omitted and that the tasks are logically and consistently related.

Again, to use the house-building example, let us look at the Design phase again:

Figure 4.4: Inputs/Deliverables for Design of House

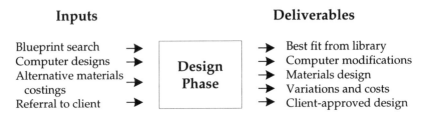

In this example, a quick check shows that each of the inputs has already been identified (no unpleasant surprises here) and each of the deliverables is "consumed" within this phase or feeds forward into the next phase, construction.

Case Study

Sue is the Remedial Services Manager for Smithtown Traveller Project.

Sue resolved that, in her piloting of an approach to improving the quality of education for traveller children, she would rely especially on the input from their families. She engaged a firm of consultants who had considerable experience in the conduct of group research involving families. When they finished their work on time, Sue was happy that they had:

- *Successfully conducted group sessions*

- *Made a full verbatim report and analysis, and*

- *Provided a plan to utilise the inputs from group discussion in the design of the traveller programme.*

However, it was only at a later stage that Sue discovered there was a gap in her WBS: the participating families wanted feedback. They were impatient to hear what use was going to be made of their ideas. After all, they had spent a lot of time and made lots of suggestions. Attending the group sessions raised their expectations, and now they wanted answers about what was going to be put in place as a result.

But by now the consultants were gone, and no further deliverable had been planned to link the focus group session outputs back into the chain. Sue was surprised to learn that the families were becoming frustrated because they had received no specific feedback. Sue thought that she had better add further subtasks covering feedback into the phase. But she had no-one assigned to do the job: the consultants had departed, and the budget was structured in such a way that she could use other private firms, but not the community workers as facilitators. She ended up having to follow up and maintain the link with the families herself, which distracted her from other work. She was glad to have recognised early in the project, though, the importance of:

- *Bringing the end clients in on the preparation of the WBS*

- *Doing reality checks on the destination of all deliverables*

- *Loosening up the access to alternative sources of expertise, and finally,*

- *Tightening up her negotiating stance with specialist suppliers like the consultants.*

In addition to testing the internal consistency, identifying inputs and deliverables also helps managers in another important respect, that is, the *allocation of resources* to responsibilities (usually through delegation). Delegation is made much easier when both the manager and the team member are absolutely clear about the task to be delegated and/or negotiated. Identifying inputs and deliverables is exactly the sort of clarity that helps managers both to delegate to team members and to negotiate their individual responsibilities. (Chapters 9 and 11 look at negotiation and delegation in more depth.)

One of the other benefits of testing the internal consistency of the plan in this way is that it also helps to highlight where *depend-*

encies exist. In other words, if a deliverable from one part of the project is a required input for another part, then we know that the project sequence must reflect this dependent relationship. This will become critical in the next stage of the planning of the change, which is the scheduling.

Finally, the identification and use of phase/task/activity inputs and deliverables confer one final benefit on change managers: it allows them to perform a rough team plan check and strategic risk check. The following questions might help in this:

- Do I have all the necessary human resources (inputs) to produce all the identified deliverables?

- Does each team member know exactly which deliverable(s) they are responsible for, either individually or collectively with other team members?

- Does each team member have the same understanding as I do about the inputs required for each phase/task/activity (this may be critical to staying within the budget)?

- Are all the identified deliverables required for (a) further stages of the change or (b) stakeholders? If not, why are we delivering them and will the "funders" pay for them?

Chapter 5

PLANNING THE CHANGE: ESTIMATING AND SCHEDULING

INTRODUCTION

In the last chapter, we looked at planning and organising the work of change projects using Work Breakdown Structures based on different levels of planning. In this chapter, we look at the other essential aspects of planning: estimating and scheduling. This chapter is heavily reliant on some of the methods of traditional project management, methods which have been proven to contribute to the accuracy of planning for change. Estimating resources, such as time and people, and scheduling the work, using flowcharts and networks, are some of the more technical aspects of project management which can help managers to manage change. If you have time and access to the appropriate technology, project management software can take some of the pain out of estimating and scheduling (such as Microsoft Project, which is relatively inexpensive). However, software is not necessary for effective change project management and, in this chapter, we will show how you can estimate and schedule the work of your change project with relative ease using the old-fashioned methods of pens-and-paper and teamwork.

ESTIMATING TIME REQUIREMENTS

Have you ever had the experience of having pressure put on you by a senior manager or by clients who are demanding that you tell them exactly when an important piece of work will be ready? You know they are waiting for it but you also know that it needs a lot more work before it will be ready. What do you do? Do you aim to please your manager or client by giving them an optimistic estimate? Do you try to extract some extra help or resources by giving a pessimistic estimate? Or do you ignore these temptations and give your most realistic estimate?

In a way, the secret to getting estimates right is to do all of the above, that is, to deliberately calculate the best estimate, the worst estimate and the most likely estimate. Although this sounds like extra work, you have automatically increased your chance of getting the estimate right because you have now defined a range rather than a single point in time. The problem with giving an estimate which is a single point in time (usually a date such as 31-Dec-1999) is that you only ever have a 50 per cent chance of being accurate — your change may actually be implemented on the right day (100 per cent accuracy) or it may not (0 per cent accuracy). (There is a technique available which allows for the exact calculation of probability in relation to estimates — in other words, it can tell you whether your estimates have a 20 per cent chance of being right or an 80 per cent chance. This technique is statistically based and is reasonably complex. Full details of how to calculate probability in this way are included as an Appendix to this book.)

If you are an experienced project manager, you will probably have run into the following pressures which militate against effective and accurate estimating of the duration of change projects:

- Clients and senior managers want a single point estimate because they do not understand the uncertainty inherent in projects

- Senior managers believe that "projects never come in on time anyhow"

- "Time is money" so people want to hear the shortest estimate rather than the most likely one

- There is greater pressure to "get it started" (i.e. the implementation of the change) rather than to spend too much time planning.

Estimating using ranges is safer and gives a fairer picture than single-point estimates. The further away a task is in time, the wider the estimation range will be. As you get closer to the task, you will be more knowledgeable about the real resource requirements and so you can refine your estimate to a much smaller range.

Most change project estimation is based on estimates of duration (hours/days/weeks, etc.) or on estimates of effort (person-hours, workdays, etc.). It is best to use one of these bases only and to be consistent throughout. Unless you are involved in very detailed estimation, our recommendation is to use duration as it makes fewer assumptions about the people who will actually do the work.

Here are some tips for improving the accuracy of estimates:

1. Start estimating from the *lowest level of detail* available to you (e.g. the task or activity level) and build upwards — it is always easier to estimate the size or duration of smaller things than bigger things.

2. In general, the person responsible for completing the task is the *best person to estimate* how long it will take (you, as manager, may then need to negotiate this estimate downwards, of course).

3. Look at every task in turn and identify the known factors and the unknown factors involved in completing that task (for example, the *known* factors might relate to familiarity with the skills required to do the job, to experience on other comparable jobs, and to the availability of a key contact person, whereas the *unknowns* might relate to the fact that the key contact person is new to the organisation and, therefore, might take longer to do their bit of it or to the fact that new technology is involved or the scale of this job is significantly bigger than previous ones).

4. Look for ways in which you can make *pro-rata extrapolations* (for example, if it took one person 10 days to produce a docu-

ment, can you assume that, if you had two people, it would take five?). However, in doing this, make sure to check the assumptions you are making about the interchangeability of resources.

5. Let everyone know that estimates will be *recorded and compared* with actual times throughout the whole project — in other words, a record of the estimates which have been agreed for each phase of the project is a major output from this part of your management of the change.

6. *Involve* as many of your team as possible in the estimating. It will encourage team members to take "ownership" of their part in the estimates and the more heads that are involved, the more perspectives you are likely to get.

TAKING ACCOUNT OF CIRCUMSTANCES

It may seem strange how often even experienced change managers get their estimates wrong. As we have mentioned, this may be due to the politics involved (wanting to give senior managers a good — if over-optimistic — estimate). However, even when managers are as truthful as possible, their estimates may still go wrong if they have failed to take the circumstances of the change team into account. Circumstantial factors, which may be beyond the immediate control of a manager, can play an important part and need to be considered.

The following is a set of *ideal* circumstances for any change project:

- A small team (no more than seven team members) who are used to working together

- The team works in the same location, preferably in the same area and at the same time

- All team members work exclusively on this one change and are fully competent and interchangeable

- The change is clearly defined and well understood by all the team members

- The team does not have to share any of its resources (people, equipment, space, etc.) with any other part of the organisation

- There are no unpredictable changes to the scope of the change project

- There is good support for the change from senior managers and from the organisation, including rapid decision-making when necessary

- The team has been involved from the start and each team member interacts with the clients.

Most change projects have to cope with one or more alterations to these factors during its course. Any deviation from the above "ideal conditions" may cause the estimates to be out. The more deviations there are, the more the estimates are likely to be understated.

The amount of time that is added on to the estimate of duration to take account of deviations from the ideal circumstances is at the discretion and judgement of individual managers and their teams (there are no logarithms to help calculate it). Of course, any time that is added on will have to be explained and negotiated with clients at the early stages. Otherwise there is a real risk that you will be forced to increase the cost and/or compromise on the quality of the change.

Our advice is that when you have completed your estimate of the duration of the change project, you build in a written clause to this estimate which takes explicit account of the circumstances which you assume will prevail during the course of the entire project. Then, if these circumstances change, you are in a better position to re-negotiate the estimate with your key stakeholders.

SCHEDULING

Scheduling is one of the primary tools which a change manager can use to manage time. Delays on project deadlines are bad news for lots of reasons: they usually impact on cost and/or quality, they cause loss of credibility, they create bad feeling between you and your clients.

Within projects, smaller delays are also unwelcome because, to avoid pushing the whole project back, they have to be absorbed and their effect on the scheduling of all future tasks has to be managed. It is easy to conclude that methods which help managers to manage their time are widely employed and a necessary part of the management of all change projects.

As mentioned earlier, this is the part of project management that is often most loved by the "technophiles". There are a number of highly sophisticated methodologies available for helping to schedule change projects. We will look at relatively "basic" versions of these methodologies which should be sufficient to help you to accurately schedule your change.

The two most common methods for scheduling projects are, in order of sophistication:

- Gantt charts (and other histograms) and

- Networking or Critical Path Analysis (CPA).

We recommend that you only use networking or CPA if your change project is very large and complex and requires a significant amount of detailed planning and resource allocation.

Gantt Charts

Henry Gantt was an Ordnance Engineer in the US Army who invented these charts in order to help him to keep track of progress in large construction projects (you will have realised by now that traditional project management owes a great deal to engineering and construction, so Gantt's occupation will come as no great surprise!).

In essence, Gantt charts are relatively simple ways of checking planned progress against actual progress. They are excellent for tracking elapsed time on straightforward or familiar projects (i.e. projects of less than 50 tasks). The charts show clearly the time relationship of tasks so, in time-critical projects, they are often all that is needed.

To construct a Gantt chart for a change project, you will need to have the following:

1. A start and end date for the project

2. A list of the tasks involved in the project

3. A sequence for the start and completion of these tasks

4. An estimate of the most probable duration of each task.

A very simple demonstration of a project Gantt chart appears below. In this project, there are only four tasks planned (A to D), each task must follow the preceding task, each one is one week long (5 working days), and the total project duration is four weeks:

Figure 5.1: A Simple Gantt Chart

Task	Duration (days)	Preceding Task(s)	Week 1	Week 2	Week 3	Week 4
Start	0					
A	5		←——→			
B	5	A		←——→		
C	5	B			←——→	
D	5	C				←——→
Finish	0					

This chart only represents the *plan*. It will have much greater value when the *actual* time required to complete each task is also entered.

If, for example, we discover that Task A started 1.5 days late (but has taken only 3.5 working days to complete) and Task B has taken 7 days, we are presented with some decisions: should we only allow three days for Task C (to bring ourselves back on schedule), should we allow four days each for the remaining two tasks, or should we re-negotiate the finish date?

The Gantt chart will not answer these questions but it does give us as much time as possible to make our decision. In Figure 5.2 below, we can see that the problem was solved by splitting the time left in the project between the last two tasks.

Figure 5.2: Gantt Chart Showing Planned vs. Actual Times for Tasks

Task	Duration (days)	Preceding Task(s)	Week 1	Week 2	Week 3	Week 4
Start	0					
A	5 3.5					
B	5 7	A				
C	5 4	B				
D	5 4	C				
Finish	0					

◄——► = planned   ◄····► = actual

The Gantt chart, therefore, acts as an early warning system. The above example is so simple that, in this case, we may not have needed a Gantt chart to provide this warning. However, you can imagine how much value early warning has when you have a project comprising several phases, each of which is made up of several tasks, or when you are managing a number of phases or even projects simultaneously.

However, one of the main shortcomings with Gantt charts is that they will not really tell you where the links or dependencies between tasks are weak. The management of this area of linkage between tasks is a major factor in good change management — you need to watch for instances where, for example, the person doing Task B does not communicate well with the person doing Task C and so there is a poor "handover" between them and time is lost. It is exactly like a relay race: the individual runners may be Olympic champions but any problems in passing the baton between them can cause all of you to lose.

An alternative to Gantt charts is networking which solves some of these difficulties although it does require a much greater investment of time. As mentioned earlier, this investment is not necessary for all projects.

NETWORKING AND CRITICAL PATHS

Network planning is a technique that shows, in diagram form, the tasks entailed in the project and how these tasks relate to each other. Network diagrams arrange all of the tasks into a logical order and show, for each task, which one(s) must come before it and which one(s) come after it. Therefore, task *interdependency* is more obvious and, in general, the more interdependency there is, the more attention must be paid to managing the links between tasks.

Network planning has several advantages over Gantt charts. It is better at showing dependencies and, in particular, it can distinguish between critical and non-critical tasks, which is a considerable aid to decision-making. Critical tasks are those tasks which, if not completed on time, will cause the whole project to be delayed unless additional resources can be invested (time and/or people) to recover the slippage, and non-critical ones are those which can be delayed *without necessarily* impacting on the overall project deadline.

The distinction between critical and non-critical tasks can also help you when you are deciding on your priorities, both at the beginning of the project and during it, should there be alterations to your circumstances.

Once the critical tasks are identified, a *critical path* can be plotted through the project. This critical path represents the longest sequence of tasks through the project which implies that any delay to these tasks delays the whole project.

Figure 5.3: Sample Network Showing Dependencies Between Tasks A to L

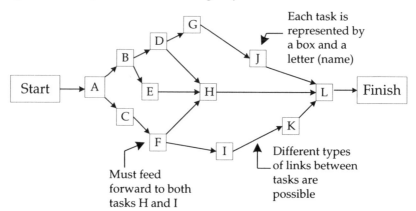

Here are some "rules" which relate to constructing networks:

1. Identify all tasks required for completion of the network

2. Relate these tasks to each other in terms of which should come first, second, third and so on, and which can be done simultaneously (given your available resources)

3. Use logic, not time or "what we usually do", to relate the tasks to each other — a useful tip here is to write each task on a separate piece of paper or "post-it"-type notes and, with your team, arrange (and re-arrange) these pieces of paper or sticky labels until you get the order right

4. Remember that the network is based on a logical sequence, not a calendar — for example, in Figure 5.3 above, it appears as if tasks D, E and F occur simultaneously but this is not necessarily the case as all the diagram is saying is that they follow B or C and precede G, H or I

5. Follow the diagramming conventions above: have a Start and Finish box and ensure that all tasks have a line coming in to them (from an earlier task or from the Start box) and a line going to another box (either a Task box or the Finish box)

6. Use the same types of links throughout the network — e.g. finish-to-start links (as shown in Figure 5.3)

7. Use "dummy links" to represent necessary lags (unavoidable or planned delays) between tasks — for example, in Figure 5.3 let us assume that task F represents ordering some equipment and task K represents the installation of that equipment: "task" I is a dummy task representing a wait of 60 days which is the time lag required to fill the order.

It should be noted that most computer software for project management will create these networks for you (once all of the necessary information has been inputted, of course).

To calculate the critical path for the network in Figure 5.3, we need to find out the longest possible sequence of linked tasks in the network, as shown in Figure 5.4 below.

Figure 5.4: Network with Durations

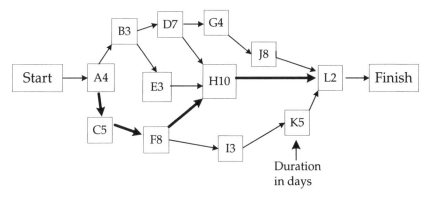

In this network, we can see that the critical path is A → C → F → H → L (total duration: 29 days). No other path through the network, following the given dependency sequence, could take longer. This path is marked with a heavy line (this is the normal convention for indicating the critical path). Any delay in any one of these tasks will affect all subsequent tasks and, unless corrective action is taken, will cause the project itself to overrun.

An important issue arises for managers once the critical path has been identified. For many managers, there is a temptation to alter the critical path by changing the durations of some of the tasks. In general, this is a bad idea as it will only result in putting yourself and your team under pressure once the project starts.

The best way to manage the critical path is to try to make it "less" critical by anticipating some of the later critical work and reassigning some of it to team members who are occupied with non-critical tasks. This perhaps sounds illogical because it seems to contradict the notion of precedence on which the network is based. In practice, it is often easy to do the groundwork for future critical tasks earlier than the network suggests.

If you are delayed on a critical task, try to resist the temptation to allocate more staff to it. Experience suggests that this does not always save time unless the "new" staff have spare time at that moment and are able to contribute effectively to the problematic critical task without requiring any extra investment of time or resources for briefing/training, etc.

IDENTIFYING FLOAT OR SPARE CAPACITY

Float refers to the amount of time around any non-critical task which can be added to the duration of that task without having any impact on the critical path or overall duration of the project (remember, critical tasks have no float). Put simply, it is the spare time available to complete that task. Float is very useful to a project manager because it can be used to allocate critical activities to team members who are working on non-critical activities and it can be used to "hide" any underestimations of duration.

Float can be calculated from a network diagram once the total duration of the critical path is known. To calculate the float for any of the non-critical tasks on the network in Figure 5.4, we need to find the longest path between start and finish which covers the relevant activity and then find out the difference between the duration of this path and the critical path.

So, for example, the float for Task D in Figure 5.4 is one day as the duration of the longest path which includes Task D is 28 days, just one day less than the critical path. Similarly, for Task E, the float is seven days and, for Task J, it is one day.

GANTTS, NETWORKS OR BOTH?

Just as Gantt charts are useful tools to help the project manager, so also are networks. However, neither is perfect and both involve some costs. Choosing between them may not be easy, especially if you are pressed for time.

The following table might make this choice easier as it summarises the main advantages and disadvantages of both Gantt charts and networks:

Table 5.5: A Comparison of Gantt Charts and Networks

Gantt Chart	Network
Relatively simple to construct and use.	Can be difficult and time-consuming to construct and use — once constructed, the network can become the "God" of the project plan.
Gives very clear indication of time elapsed and progress over time.	Shows logical sequence of tasks in project — it is often hard to read and should not be used to record progress over time.
Does not show dependencies and links between tasks very well.	Excellent for highlighting critical path and, therefore, for helping project manager to prioritise and anticipate.

If this has not made your choice much easier, perhaps it is because you would prefer to use both tools. This is very common — in fact, it is unusual to see networks being used without Gantt charts (although less unusual the other way around). Bear in mind that both are tools to help you *plan and schedule only* — they will not necessarily help you to communicate or make decisions and they should be regularly updated to account for variations and alterations to your change project. In any event, they are both based on estimates only. If short of time, the wise change manager will invest extra time in getting the estimates right rather than getting the Gantt chart or network right.

Extract from Interview —
Project Manager, Financial Services Company

"How did you go about planning the launch of the product?"

"Well, we knew all our parameters early on — the amount of time we had, the budget, and the sales targets and some of the other quality aspects. I had been involved peripherally in the launch of another product so I had some idea of the sorts of things that would have to happen to have us ready on time for the launch date. At the stage where the planning took place, only three of us were on board. I drew up a blueprint of the whole process as I saw it and we spent half a day initially, using that blueprint as a basis, trying to identify all of the things that needed to be done in the nine-month run-up to the launch date."

"How did you draw up that blueprint?"

"To a degree, it was intuition. I said to myself that, within three months, I wanted the basics of a computer system in place, within six months I wanted the full team on board and fully involved as well as some computer testing using mock business, and the final three month period would be the rest of the recruitment, more intensive training and problem-solving, testing and trouble-shooting the systems, designing the manual. So it was a case of just figuring out what needs to be done first, which bit was contingent on other bits."

"And was this amended much?"

"Yes, quite considerably. It's amazing how much you can forget or overlook. When the three of us sat down at the planning meeting, we thought of a lot more things that needed to be done within the three-month phases that I had sketched out. So we put flesh on the bones of the blueprint and went into quite a bit of detail on the various aspects. This was good because we saw that things which, say, I'd put in the final phases, like recruitment, had to start much earlier in order to actually happen when we needed them to happen. Recruitment is a good example, because unless you're recruiting internally, you have to allow for the fact that the people might have notice periods to work out so you actually need to be able to make a job offer about two months, or even three, before you actually need the person on board. The same with PR — in order to have PR at the time you need it, you have to start much earlier. What ended up happening was that the first and second three-month phases were much more crowded than I had initially allowed for in the blueprint.

Then there were other amendments because when we had identified all the activities, it became very clear that nearly all of them were contingent on something else happening first. So things had to be moved around a lot to allow for that as there were just the three of us and that was the way it stayed until about four months in. In our initial planning we also looked at contingency plans in the event of major breakdowns or cock-ups — we identified about six doomsday scenarios, like computer breakdowns, or software problems, or key contacts in our UK parent company leaving, and looked at what would happen the plan if any of these were to actually happen. This allowed us to see that, in fact, the whole launch would not take place if two of these doomsday events were to happen so it concentrated my mind on making sure as far as I could that they didn't.

When we were happy that we had the plan right, it went to senior management here in Ireland and also in the UK and the UK made a few changes, but nothing major. In the plan that we sent up to the UK, I had put in some estimates of how the budget would be spent over the nine months and I think they were happy with that part, particularly because they saw that we knew what we were doing and that it all seemed to be manageable both in terms of getting everything done on time and within the overall budget that they had set aside. They didn't really interfere in any aspect of the management of the launch and they made it quite clear that they were giving me a lot of discretion but, nonetheless, it didn't hurt to have them 'approve' the plan with its outline costings for the major aspects like IT, staffing, etc."

"And during the nine-month launch period, were there other changes?"

"Well, inevitably, I suppose, not everything happened according to the plan. One semi-doomsday scenario arose that none of us predicted and it threw us off course for about a month and, yeah, there were lots of smaller deviations too. But the plan still remained as the kind of map for the whole thing. There were probably more deviations in the budget side than in the dates."

"Did you use software to help you to draw up the plan?"

"No, well, nothing over and above just spreadsheets and word-processing and that kind of thing. But no, we didn't have access to any of the really sophisticated packages — I don't think any of us could have used them even if we did. They probably would have helped, especially when changes had to be made because the final document had so much tippex and stuff on it that it became hard to read, especially as an early change would have knock-on effects on lots of the activities that were scheduled for the later phases. Yeah, on reflection, if I were doing it all again, I probably would investigate the software in more detail or maybe include in the staffing budget someone who was familiar with it and could use it to draw up the overall plan."

Chapter 6

PLANNING THE CHANGE: RESOURCE BUDGETING

INTRODUCTION

We saw (when looking at the initiation of change projects, in Chapter 2) that one of the three critical dimensions of the management of change projects is cost. It is estimated that one in every three projects does not finish on target in respect of cost. Yet, in many organisations, a manager's performance is implicitly evaluated on their ability to budget and to manage a budget. If managers meet or come in on budget, they are assumed to be doing a good job, if they exceed their budget, they are often judged as being deficient in their management capacity (regardless of their ability to deliver the right results).

Much of this chapter will concentrate on planning for the use and control of human resources as it is people who usually account for the vast bulk of expenditure (on non-capital change projects). In fact, in the terminology of traditional project management, "resources" is often synonymous with "people". We will follow this convention too in this chapter.

RESPONSIBILITY ACCOUNTING

As manager, you are likely to be held responsible for the overall achievement of the change project objectives within budget, on time and to the required specification. This may seem to be an unfair burden, as many of the variables which affect your chances of this achievement may be beyond your control.

It makes sense, therefore, for you, as manager, to be fully aware of which costs you will be held accountable for. For example, would you be held accountable for a cost overrun that was caused by exchange rate fluctuations or sick leave?

The general principle here is that you should try to negotiate at the start of the change project for "responsibility accounting" which means that you should only be responsible for those costs which you can be reasonably expected to control. This principle underlies our earlier advice, for example, to document the circumstantial assumptions which you make in compiling your estimates for the duration of different parts of the change project. It is worthwhile, therefore, to spend some time at the beginning of the project making a distinction between controllable costs and costs which are not controllable but which may, nonetheless, affect your project.

In addition to the alterations to circumstantial factors which we discussed in Chapter 5, the following are common reasons behind cost overruns on change projects:

- Costs of replacing key personnel who leave the project

- Overtime payments (e.g. caused by sickness)

- Equipment, especially IT equipment, problems or breakdowns or repair/replacement costs

- Exchange rate or interest rate fluctuations

- Maternity leave replacement costs

- Training costs (if trained personnel are not available).

The causes of cost overruns may well be beyond your control but, nonetheless, you may be expected to amend your budget for the change to compensate for such overruns — in other words, savings may have to be made on later phases to "soak up" the earlier overrun. Alternatively, you may have to negotiate a "contingency budget" with your funders.

In addition to identifying uncontrollable costs, managers need to establish at the beginning which *direct* costs and which *indirect* costs are to be attributed to their change. Direct costs are costs which vary with usage — the more you use, the more it costs — and indirect costs are ones which are incurred regardless of usage. An example of a typical direct cost would be consultancy fees, overtime or office rent, and typical indirect costs would be basic salaries (without overtime) and overhead allocations for central organisational costs such as an allocation for "management over-head" or "depreciation overhead".

Costs may vary between change projects. For example, will the project use a room in an office building and, if so, will a wear-and-tear occupation overhead (an indirect cost) be charged? Or will the project rent its own office space and pay rent by the square metre (a direct cost)? What about the use of electricity and other utilities: are these to be charged directly to the project or will a blanket "utilities overhead" be charged? Will communications costs be charged directly or on an overhead basis? The reason why you need to think about these costs is because you may, if necessary, be able to reduce the direct costs (by cutting back on usage), but it is much more difficult to make any impact on indirect costs.

In a way, it helps to think of the change as a separate "business entity". If you were running this project as your own business or company, what would you expect to pay for? This will give some idea of the sorts of questions you need to ask, as somebody is paying for all of these "hidden" costs and, if this "somebody" is you, as manager, you need to know this early enough so that you can budget for them.

Case Study — The Overseas Aid Change Project

In one case, a consultant who was brought in to manage a change project was given an "in-kind" donation of furnished office space for his team. The local Government had persuaded a businessman to provide the space in his company's offices. The office furniture included a state-of-the art computer. The team's new office itself consisted of four rooms in the commercial part of town. The team members were delighted with their free offices and were full of suggestions as to how the money they had saved on office rental might be spent. It was agreed that the money would be spent on extending the pilot site for the change project and the plans were accordingly amended.

Unfortunately, just two months into the change, the manager received an internal invoice from the accounts branch of the company which was providing the office space. It seemed that, although no rent was to be charged, the project was liable for the overhead costs associated with the office space. It transpired that the project budget had to cover a depreciation charge on the new computer, a "wear-and-tear" charge on the office and a blanket overhead charge for air conditioning and electricity. Worse still, these overheads were calculated on the basis of square metres in occupation so the project, with its four large rooms, was particularly hard hit, especially as the team could easily have managed with just two rooms. Worse again was the fact that the team had already announced its extension of the pilot site and would have to continue on this extended basis. The manager did not know how they would now pay for this.

He swore to himself that he would never be stung like this again. In the future, he would not make plans without budgeting very carefully for all of the costs which he might have to cover.

BUDGETING AND RESOURCE ALLOCATION

A budget is the primary way in which the change manager will seek to plan and control the costs of any change project. You do not have to be an accountant to prepare a project budget. It often helps to think of a budget as being simply the equivalent of a plan with a price tag attached. In the last chapter, we looked in some detail at the planning part, so now we have to attach the price tag.

At a minimum, the budget for the project should clearly identify everything that the project will have to pay for. For example, this might include salaries, office rental or accommodation, communications, travel and subsistence, consultancy fees, insurance, equipment purchase or rental, materials, printing, etc.

A key part of budgeting is the necessity to *make assumptions* about what resources (i.e. people, for the most part) will cost in the future based on their current price. We make assumptions all the time when planning so the budgeting process is no different. However, because budgets are so sensitive and because there is likely to be so much stakeholder interest in this aspect of your management, our advice is that you document each and every assumption you make in the preparation of your budget. This means, for example, that if you assume that it will take somebody five days to complete a critical path task, you are making several implicit assumptions about that person's capacity. This is a common area for problems in management because, as we know, one person's ability to do a job may vary dramatically from another person's ability.

The solution here would be to make a record of your assumption, i.e. "Task X: estimated to take a (*fully-trained, competent*) person five days @ £100 per day" or "Task X: estimated to take (*person's name*) five days @ £100 per day". This will allow you much greater control over your change as any alteration to the resource will then send you a message that your assumption is no longer valid and that the task may take longer to complete which may have an adverse impact on your budget.

Much of the success of budgeting relates to two factors: firstly, as we have just seen, it relates to resource performance or competence and, secondly, it relates to the accuracy of the schedules which you have already completed. To summarise, there are a number of steps which you need to go through to ensure that your budget is as good as it can be. The first part of the exercise relates to the *costing* of activities and the second part relates to ensuring that resources are efficiently *allocated*.

1. Steps in Costing the Project

1. Complete a Work Breakdown Structure (WBS)

2. Identify the resources you need to complete each activity or task of the WBS (resources can be identified by name if you already know the composition of your team or they can be identified by skill type — e.g. IT specialist, administrative assistant, trainer, etc.). Cost each resource based on existing or generic information (e.g. actual salary cost to date, salary of similar grade workers, etc.).

3. Make an estimate of the cost of each task based on a cost-per-day (or per-week, if more appropriate) per resource.

4. Consider all the additional costs associated with each task (e.g. materials, communications, outside expertise, travel, etc.) and then, for each task, sum all of the costs.

5. Add the sum of all of the task costs to get the total phase costs, and add the sum of the phase costs to get the total cost. Making these sums cumulative is usually the easiest way (see worked example later in this chapter).

6. You may find that it makes more sense to allocate indirect costs on a simple pro-rata basis across the entire project — for example, if phase 1 of the change is estimated to take 15 per cent of the project duration, 15 per cent of the total overhead cost may be attributed to phase 1. However, remember not to try to "cut corners" by doing this for direct costs!

So far, the budgeting process is relatively straightforward. It is mostly a matter of accurate allocation and simple arithmetic. For large change projects, a computer spreadsheet will make this even easier.

However, the real benefit of budgeting relates not to the simple costing of activities but to the second part, that is, the examination of whether you have allocated resources in the most efficient manner. In other words, can you afford the right resources in the right quantities at the right time or can you re-arrange things so that you can get the job done without spending more?

2. Checking and Allocating Resources

1. Consider the nature of your resources: are you likely to have a full-time change team or will you have a team composed of key resources as and when you require them (i.e. "resources on tap"). If your team is full-time, you need to check how each resource is to be used throughout the change project. Are there times when your schedule suggests that a key team member needs to work 120 hours per week and other times when this resource is idle? If your resources are "on tap", are they available in the right quantity and how much notice do they need?

2. If you find that you have resource over-allocation or under-allocation (e.g. 120 hour weeks versus 20 hour weeks), your next job is to try to reallocate your resources so that their working weeks are more balanced. In particular, you should look at all your critical path activities: do you have the required resources in the required amounts to be able to complete these tasks on time? If you have significant over-allocation on critical path tasks (i.e. you find you have a key resource person working 120-hour weeks during the critical times), you may run into difficulty in your change unless you can make other resources available to assist at these critical times.

3. Look at all the non-critical activities and assess the amount of float around each one: can you move tasks so that you get a more efficient use of resources? Alternatively, can you employ resources on other tasks if they are idle?

There are very few absolute rules to help change managers re-allocate resources, other than the ones already mentioned. However, if you do encounter problems in resource allocation, here is a summary of some tips which may help:

*   Shorten the duration of the critical path by reducing the quality of the output or deliverable that is required from some

tasks or from each task (if you do this, remember to think about the implications of lesser quality on later phases of the change).

- Re-deploy resources within their available float.

- Examine the critical activities: can any part of them be brought forward or prepared in advance so that they can be completed in a shorter time?

- Train other members of the team so that they can help out more effectively at critical times.

- Accept that you have an over-allocation on certain critical activities and make savings elsewhere (especially on non-critical activities) so that you can afford the over-allocation.

- See if you can find cheaper team members who have the same level of competence.

Of course, only you, as manager, can make these judgements. Decisions such as these are likely to be political and to have other implications for the project.

CONTROLLING THE BUDGET

As mentioned earlier, stakeholders tend to take a particular interest in the budget or cost side of management. For this reason, and because it is good management practice too, it makes sense to plan and control financial performance quite carefully throughout the change.

There are a few simple but effective ways in which you can help yourself to control your budget. The first of these ways concerns setting *tolerable variances* between planned expenditure and actual expenditure. In a way, this is a bit like constructing a financial Gantt chart. The purpose is also the same as that of a Gantt chart, i.e. to give yourself early warning of problems. However, the beauty of having identified tolerable variances is that you do not need early warning of all variances, only ones which are really likely to cause you problems if they were to go unchecked.

For instance, a variance of just one per cent on the budget of a major critical task could amount to a significant sum of money but one per cent on another task might not be a problem at all. Thinking in advance about tolerable variances is, therefore, a way of "setting a budget alarm clock" for yourself.

Below are some simple tables showing how a manager might manage the budget. Imagine the change concerns the renovation of an old building on a university campus and its conversion to a library. The preliminary estimate of days for this project is shown in Table 6.1.

Table 6.1: Estimate of Duration

Project: Renovation of Library						
	Phase of Project					
Team Member	**1**	**2**	**3**	**4**	**5**	**6**
Manager	23	22	8	30	24	45
Architect	40	40	32	16	16	32
Conservation Specialist	30	30	20	20	20	30
Engineer	10	5	5	0	0	0
Quantity Surveyor	40	40	40	40	40	40
Fire Consultant	10	10	20	20	20	30
Support staff	10	5	5	5	0	20
Total Days	163	152	130	131	120	197

This resource estimate is costed by simply multiplying the daily cost per resource type and summing for each phase. The manager has calculated these phase costs as shown in Table 6.2.

Table 6.2: Estimate of Cost

Project: Renovation of Library						
	Estimated Resource Cost per Phase (£000)					
Team Member	**1**	**2**	**3**	**4**	**5**	**6**
Manager	5.1	4.8	1.7	6.6	5.3	9.9
Architect	8.0	8.0	6.4	3.2	3.2	6.4
Conservation Specialist	3.6	3.6	2.4	2.4	2.4	3.6
Engineer	2.0	1.0	1.0	0.0	0.0	0.0
Quantity Surveyor	6.0	6.0	6.0	6.0	6.0	6.0
Fire Consultant	1.8	1.8	3.6	3.6	3.6	3.6
Support staff	1.0	0.5	0.5	0.5	0.0	2.0
Total Cost/Phase	27.5	25.7	21.6	22.3	20.8	32.1
Cumulative Project Cost	27.5	53.2	74.8	97.1	117.9	150.0

Let us suppose that the project is almost half-way into its life and the manager wants to see how he is doing with regard to his budget. At this stage, he knows what he planned as expenditure for each of the three complete phases and he now knows his actual expenditure on these phases. As this is his first change project, he has set a 0 per cent variance toleration — in other words, he wants to know about all variances between budgeted expenditure and actual expenditure with regard to resource usage. Table 6.3 is an example of how the manager's budget reports might look for the first three phases of the project.

Table 6.3: Budgeted versus Actual Cost

Team Member	Phase 1 — Budget v. Actual		Phase 2 — Budget v. Actual		Phase 3 — Budget v. Actual		Total Var.
Project: Renovation of Library							
Resource Usage: Variance per Phase (£000)							
Manager	5.1	5.2	4.8	4.9	1.7	1.9	+0.4
Architect	8.0	8.0	8.0	8.3	6.4	6.2	+0.1
Conservation Specialist	3.6	3.6	3.6	4.0	2.4	3.4	+1.4
Engineer	2.0	1.1	1.0	1.1	1.0	0.8	-1.0
Quantity Surveyor	6.0	6.9	6.0	6.1	6.0	6.1	+1.1
Fire Consultant	1.8	0.7	1.8	0.8	7.2	7.2	-2.1
Support staff	1.0	0.4	0.5	0.7	0.5	2.0	+1.1
Total Phase	27.5	25.9	25.7	25.9	21.6	24.0	
Variance (+/–)		+1.6		-0.2		-2.4	+1.0

Thus, the manager can see that things are not going exactly as planned (they rarely do!). In phases 1 and 2, he had over-budgeted for his resources — they appear to have been more productive than he had given them credit for. However, for this exercise to be truly useful to the manager, he would want to find out why variances were occurring and to start asking questions, such as:

- Has he underestimated the productivity of some of his resources (particularly the fire consultant and the engineer who seem to have cost much less than budgeted in the first two phases)?

- Has anything happened to the fire consultant or the engineer (have they been working on another building or prevented from working because of some accident on site)?

Other issues which might be signalled by the above budget reports are:

- Erroneous assumptions by the manager about the amount of time necessary to complete tasks in different phases

- Calculation errors

- Erroneous estimates of the productivity of the people concerned

- The conservation specialist has done some of the work which had been scheduled for the fire consultant — for example, they thought they would have to install an additional fire escape but the conservationist has been able to re-open a disused "servant's entrance" (which would account for the specialist's costs being higher than budgeted and the fire consultant's costs being lower than budgeted)

- Erroneous assumptions about the nature of the work required for completion of different phases

- Bad weather has caused a hold-up in some activities.

In other words, it might have been any one of a number of factors that has caused the difference. The real purpose of this kind of budgeting and checking is to prompt you to ask questions in case the answers continue to have a bearing on the rest of the project (for example, in the above project, the manager is already £1,000 over budget).

An important point here concerns the way resource costs have been treated in this example. In this change project, the staff were all full-time on this project and, therefore, the manager could have taken a short-cut and simply allocated the total salary costs to the different phases. Had he done so in this case it would be very difficult to even see any variance let alone ask the right questions about the causes of this variance. The moral of this story is to always plan and budget in detail for resource costs (even if your team members are coming to you "free") because you need the early warning system that the budget can provide.

Finally, one further point about budgeting concerns *flexing* the budget. In the above example, you can see that the Conservation Specialist's costs were higher than were expected. On examination, the manager found out that this was because this Specialist had some free time (float) in phase 3 and decided to start on one of the phase 4 tasks in phase 3. However, one of the effects of the Specialist's action is that the budget performance looks terrible and, without the explanation to account for the variance, stakeholders might form an adverse impression about how the change was being managed.

One way around this is to have flexible budgeting, whereby the budget is flexed to take account of changes to the predicted or anticipated timescale of direct costs being incurred. If we planned to incur direct labour costs in phase 4, but we actually incur them in phase 3, we keep our budget flexible so that our budget reflects the number of direct cost hours which were actually incurred in phase 3 rather than which were planned for phase 3 (and phase 4 is accordingly reduced).

Table 6.4 shows one way in which a manager might flex his budgets to account for actual labour rather than planned labour (remember, we are flexing the budget to take account of direct costs (labour or resource time) which have been incurred in a pattern which was different to the pattern we expected).

Such flexing is not only legitimate (it is *not* "creative budgeting") but sensible, otherwise your early warning system is calling your attention to changes which do not need your attention.

The variance which the manager in the above example is interested in concerns not the resource usage (the fact that the Conservation Specialist anticipated some of his phase 4 work in phase 3) but the fact that the cost for this resource has risen (as a result of her promotion at the start of phase 3) and is likely to have knock-on effects on the budget for the remainder of the change project.

Table 6.4: Explanation of Variance

Project: Renovation of Library					
Phase 3: Detail Sheet: Conservation Specialist					
Planned Days	Cost per Day (£)	Budget (£000)	Actual Days	Actual Cost per Day	Actual Cost (£000)
20	120	2.4	26.5	130	3.4

Notes: Specialist (Grade 2) was promoted to Specialist Grade 1 at start of phase 3. Budget for phase 4 flexed to take account of reduced days in phase 4.

Finally, a note on budgeting, particularly "interactive budgeting", such as flexing around direct costs: this activity is worthwhile but can be time-consuming. A computer spreadsheet package can make this exercise a great deal more efficient as you will not need to re-enter formulas (e.g. such as the formula to multiply the cost per day by the number of days to give the phase total for each resource) more than once. We strongly recommend that, if you have not already done so, you equip yourself with such a package at the start of any change project.

TROUBLESHOOTING THE BUDGET

As we have said many times in this text, a plan is an attempt to predict the future. It will not be perfect: there will always be deviations between the plan and the reality. Equally, if your budget is merely a plan with a price tag, you can expect deviations here too.

If (when) you have deviations between your planned expenditure and your actual expenditure, you will want to know why and how to "fix" it. Below is a summary of some of the most-used options available to managers if they discover that their budget is going off-course:

• Reduce the quality of some or all of the deliverables

• Reduce the length of the critical path

- Re-deploy resources from non-critical activities to delayed critical ones

- Build in some "contingency" into the funding request

- Get cheaper resources

- Get the commissioning client to contribute some additional resources or delegate some of the work to the clients or to other parts of the organisation

- Work longer hours

- Negotiate a reduced scope

- Take longer to deliver on the final deliverables, and

- (Less advisable, but a regular occurrence): don't let the stake-holders know about the budget overrun until they have seen the results of the change.

Chapter 7

CONTROLLING THE CHANGE: MEASURING AND MONITORING PERFORMANCE

INTRODUCTION

One of the acknowledged strengths of traditional project management is its inherent reliance on performance measurement and control. It will be clear to you already that key components of project management, such as planning and scheduling, have limited value unless they are used to help you to check on your progress and then to take corrective action if necessary.

This checking and modifying is, in fact, the essence of control. The diagram below shows how control works in more detail.

Figure 7.1: Cycle of Control

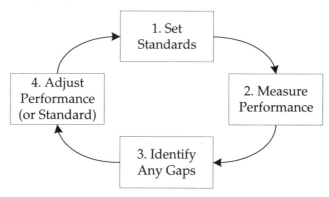

This diagram suggests that there are four key skills involved in controlling projects (or anything else):

- **Standards**: setting standards is implicit in good management. In effect, the agreement at the start of any change in relation to the specified time, cost and quality is itself a standard-setting process. Good control requires breaking down these three global standards into finer detail. The chapters on project planning include some options for doing this in relation to managing time and resources.

- **Measuring Performance**: again, one of the key strengths of project management is that, typically, it is full of tools and techniques to help measure progress against a pre-determined and agreed plan (e.g. Gantt charts). However, project management (like many other forms of management) tends to over-rely on the measurement of quantitative aspects of performance (such as time and cost).

- **Identifying Gaps**: control is largely about the management of exceptional performance and variances, rather than normal or predicted performance. It seems obvious, then, that most managers will concentrate on taking action to "fill in any gaps that arise" and let the normal on-target work take care of itself. However, for many reasons (such as organisational politics, fear, etc.), a surprisingly large number of change project reports omit any reporting of "bad news", even though serious unresolved problems were evident.

- **Adjusting performance** (to correct the gap) or **reviewing the standard** (if the standard was poorly set): in many ways, this is one of the *management* aspects of change project management. Managers and their teams are charged with delivering the required results, not with just monitoring and reporting on progress. If remedial action needs to be taken to deliver the project on time and within budget, this decision must be taken and acted on by the manager (as long as they have the authority).

WHO BENEFITS FROM CONTROL?

The simple answer to this question is that everyone involved in your change project should benefit from effective project control.

However, this may not reflect the reality of all projects. Some projects develop or adopt a culture of punishment. Control is ineffective and can be very costly if it is used to blame or punish "the usual suspects" rather than to prompt a less personal but more thorough exploration of what led to the delay, or cost overrun, or error, etc. In other words, the purpose of control is to learn from mistakes and to improve performance, by identifying problems as early as possible and devising (and implementing) the most appropriate solutions to these problems. If control is excessive, or if it leads to individuals being highlighted as the cause of the problem, the control might well be counter-productive.

Measuring and controlling performance has the following benefits:

- It acts as an early warning system, giving you and your team maximum time to take corrective action thus minimising upset to the client.

- Because it is designed to give more warning time, it can improve decision-making — generally speaking, the more time is available, the more corrective options are available and this can be a significant boon to both you and the clients.

- Regular feedback on performance, such as is provided by a good control system, is recognised to be one of the most powerful and enduring of motivators and one of the most attractive aspects of project work for all involved.

- Good change management means that resource requirements will have been negotiated and planned well in advance, but real life is often not like this. Performance measurement often provides the "heavy artillery" for managers who are involved in resource battles in organisations — it is difficult to make a case for additional resources or to fight off a raid on your existing resources without having "the figures" to support your stance.

However, beware of one of the common downfalls of traditional project management whereby the measures and controls become the "god" of the work rather than being seen for what they are — a means to an end.

PERFORMANCE INDICATORS

You will remember back when we were talking about identifying and initiating change projects (Chapter 2), we talked about the three principal performance dimensions to the scope of a change project as quality, time and cost.

You and your team must have effective control over each of these three dimensions of performance throughout the duration of the change project. As mentioned earlier, there is a temptation to monitor time and cost only because they are quantitative and generally easier to measure. However, seeking to control time and costs is not enough as no client will want a change which meets the specification in terms of deadline and budget but delivers the wrong result or the right result but to poor quality. Again, it is worth remembering that time, cost and quality are in a "sealed" relationship to each other. Overruns or shortfalls in one can only be accommodated by reducing or adding more to one or both of the others.

The following paragraphs will cover the three dimensions of performance in more detail and should help to expand the range of measures and indicators which are potentially available to managers.

Time-Related Measures

Time is the simplest of the three dimensions to measure and, by implication, to control. One reason for this is that measures of time are absolute and cross-cultural. We all use the same units to measure time (although our interpretation of some of them may vary — e.g. a "week" might represent anything from 35 to 50 hours' work). In addition, referring back to Figure 7.1, the "standard" for controlling time is also relatively easy for managers to set because the standard is the project schedule.

Gantt Charts

We discussed the use of Gantt charts and networks, two of the most commonly used tools to control time, in Chapter 5.

Gantt charts are relatively simple to construct and are particularly effective in helping to manage and control time as they give a graphic display of any gaps between actual progress over time and planned progress over time. They can, therefore, provide you with early warning of problems or difficulties and, in so doing, give you the maximum leeway in deciding how any problems should be remedied.

Milestones

Another common way to control progress over time is to use milestones, which are clearly-marked checkpoints built in to the plan which enable the team to know that they are on the right track. Milestones, therefore, should be significant testable points in the plan with clear deliverables. Milestones are designed to mark the end of different segments or phases within projects. If these milestones are reached on time, everyone knows the project is on schedule. If milestones are not reached on time, everyone knows there is a problem. Milestones are also frequently used to "sign off" on one stage of a change and to secure a decision to proceed to the next part.

Typical generic change project milestones include:

- Agreement and approval of terms of reference (including scope, budget, deadline, quality of result, etc.)

- Agreement of the plan (including Work Breakdown Structure, estimates, schedule and budget)

- Approval for diagnosis and design of solution

- Piloting of solution and agreed analysis of results of pilot including any proposals for modification to plan

- Implementation (depending on the nature of the change, implementation will normally be further segmented into phases)

- Evaluation of the entire project and approval for any recommendations based on the evaluation.

Good milestones should have a tangible deliverable. In the case of many of the milestones mentioned above, the deliverable would be a document which had been signed (approved) by the relevant parties. Milestones can mark the end of phases, the completion of tasks or even the completion of subtasks. If a phase is very long or complex, it is recommended to use task and/or subtask milestones in addition to phase-end milestones.

Milestones are useful not only in managing and controlling progress against a schedule but also in motivating the members of the project team. To get this motivation benefit, milestones should be no more than approximately three months apart and they should be celebrated or marked in some way.

Cost-Related Measures

With regard to costs, the main question relates to progress against the budget. Is the change on target in its expenditure or is a certain phase costing more than planned? Like time, cost is relatively easy to measure in that money is a reasonably stable measure and is easily understood by all.

On most change projects, the major item of expenditure throughout the project is likely to be people or "resources". A labour budget is, therefore, critical to controlling costs and is usually the "standard" for controlling expenditure.

As was discussed in Chapter 6 (Resource Budgeting), it is important that you establish from the outset what resource costs you are to manage. This means identifying and making explicit which costs in relation to which resources are to be charged to your project. You should aim to avoid the situation where you are held responsible for costs over which you have no control (e.g. exchange rate fluctuations or sickness-related payments). If you cannot avoid such situations, you should try to negotiate as much discretion as possible in relation to how you deal with such costs.

The main way in which you can seek control over expenditure is to keep a steady watch on cash flow and on cumulative expenditure throughout the project. "Money milestones" are also a good idea, in other words, clear checkpoints against which you can measure your cumulative expenditure and your output for that amount of money. Clients in particular are often reassured to see tangible outputs or deliverables especially as, for them, most of the money goes out at the beginning but most of the result comes in at the end.

As we saw in Chapter 6, variance reporting is usually the most effective way of keeping operational control of budgets. Simple bar charts, where phases or tasks are plotted against planned and actual expenditure, are often the best way to keep track of how costs are behaving over time.

Quality-Related Measures

As noted earlier, for many projects this will be the most difficult aspect to measure because quality is not as readily quantifiable as time and costs. This means that it often requires more ingenuity to find measures which adequately represent quality.

The overall quality objective of the project is the degree and type of impact which the change is to have on its clients. In some cases, certain dimensions of this impact will be relatively easily measured.

If we take some examples of change projects, the following quality indicators might be used:

Example 1: Training Programme for Front-line Staff in Customer Care
- **Indicators**: Number of staff who have completed the Programme. Response time to client-initiated contacts (e.g. telephone calls, letters, requests for assistance, etc.). Number of service problems (a) identified and (b) solved. Cost of training versus estimated cost of not training staff in customer care. Staff satisfaction with Programme.

Example 2: Introduction of a More Effective Cash Control System

- **Indicators**: Time taken to collect cash one year ago and now. Customer response to pay-prompt letters. Auditors' views on new system. Size of bank balance. Number of clients who need pay prompting. Time elapsed from delivery to invoicing to payment. Performance against benchmarks set by credit control industry regulators. Number of cash/credit control problems (a) identified and (b) solved.

Example 3: Use of Public Libraries by General Public in Local Authority Area

- **Indicators**: The number of visits per library per annum. The percentage of the total literate population which visited a public library in the past year. The percentage of the population which regularly (i.e. 6+ times per year) uses a public library. The number of first-time visitors to a public library in the past year. etc. Again, increases in any of these figures would indicate achievement of the objective.

We can see from this that it is relatively easy to find specific indicators of strength of impact for some qualitative objectives. In some cases, these indicators will relate to measures of time and cost as well.

However, in some cases, it may not be so easy to identify "statistics" such as these which can be used to measure strength of impact. If your change project is in a very new area or if you are not sure of what is driving the quality you are aiming to change, it can be quite difficult to find quantifiable indicators. Take, for example, projects in the area of health education — what indicators would tell you that you (a) were educating the right people (b) that your education of these people was causing changes in their behaviour and (c) that these changes in behaviour were causing improvements in the health of the community? This is a classic example of a quality being a consequence of:

1. Investing the right *inputs* (e.g. resources, etc.) in order to

2. Produce the right *outputs* (e.g. behaviour changes) which

3. Cause the right *outcome* (e.g. health improvement).

In this case, all three links in this quality chain need to be present for our desired impact to be achieved. Measuring 1 or 2 will not provide definitive evidence of the achievement of our outcome — in other words, simply counting up how much we spent on the education programmes or the number of people who participated in the education programme (both of which are inputs) will not tell us whether we are improving the community's health, just as measuring the amount or type of behaviour change (outputs) will not tell us either.

It is only by measuring the actual gain in health (outcome) that we will know whether we have been successful, and it is only by being able to relate the achievement of the outcome to the outputs and inputs that we can prove that it was *our* intervention that caused the improvement (and not some other coincidental variable).

The conclusion from this is that, to measure quality, it is often necessary to measure inputs, outputs and outcome. If time is of the essence, prioritise by trying to measure the outcome or, to begin with, a small selection of inputs/outputs in addition to the outcome, as shown in Figure 7.2.

Figure 7.2: Three Aspects of Getting Quality Right

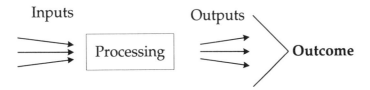

MEASURING CONSUMER RESPONSE

In many cases, measuring outcomes means measuring the impact of our efforts on the consumers of our products or services. In the example above, we might have measured the health gain or benefit by reference to World Health Organisation standards for community health status. However, another way in which we could have assessed the impact of our work would be to devise a scale or questionnaire on the perceived health of the community. Very often, these scales and questionnaires do not have to be very elaborate and you do not always need sophisticated statistical analyses of the results to draw valid conclusions.

Some of the most effective ways of measuring impact are simple "before" versus "after" ratings (out of 10 or 100) by the target population on differential scales that the population itself defines as meaningful. This means that it is not the "experts" who define whether the change has been beneficial, but the clients themselves. This is possibly the best way of ensuring quality because it is the consumers who define what quality means for them in relation to the particular "product" which you are supplying.

Some examples of differential scales which might be used to measure quality in relation to the provision of a telephone back-up support service to purchasers of new computers are shown overleaf in Figure 7.3. The customers themselves, in an earlier telephone survey, defined these issues as key measures of the quality of the service.

It is clear that such scales do not meet all of the requirements for full statistical analysis — they are, by design, interpretative rather than absolute. However, changes in overall ratings, following implementation of the change, provide powerful evidence that the desired impact has been achieved (or not). In terms of managing stakeholders, commissioning clients are often more impressed by changes on unsophisticated but highly relevant scales, such as the ones above, than they are by super-sophisticated but less relevant statistics.

Figure 7.3: Example of Differential Scales to Measure Quality of Telephone Survey

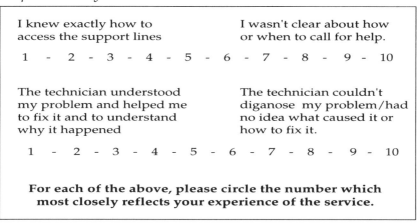

> I knew exactly how to access the support lines
>
> I wasn't clear about how or when to call for help.
>
> 1 - 2 - 3 - 4 - 5 - 6 - 7 - 8 - 9 - 10
>
> The technician understood my problem and helped me to fix it and to understand why it happened
>
> The technician couldn't diganose my problem/had no idea what caused it or how to fix it.
>
> 1 - 2 - 3 - 4 - 5 - 6 - 7 - 8 - 9 - 10
>
> **For each of the above, please circle the number which most closely reflects your experience of the service.**

In general, there are a number of dimensions of quality that people usually rate as important. These dimensions are generic and, to a greater or lesser extent, can be used, therefore, in the measurement of all change. By including some of these in your measurement of quality, you will get a more complete perspective of the level and type of impact which your change is delivering. The dimensions include:

- Economy — did the change incur unnecessary financial resources?

- Efficiency — did you get a good ratio of outputs for your investment of inputs?

- Effectiveness — is the outcome the appropriate one for the target population?

- Relevance — was the outcome relevant and meaningful to the target group as a whole or would they have preferred that the money was spent on something else?

- Access — did the change make for easier access/ease of use?

- Reliability

- Durability

- Flexibility

- Creativity

- Customisation to client needs.

PROCEDURES FOR MONITORING AND CONTROLLING

There are a number of tried-and-tested methods for monitoring and controlling change. Traditional project management is, however, rightly criticised for over-relying on these methods so it is worth remembering that the method is only as good as the people who are using it. In addition, monitoring and control will be practised only if people can see a benefit from them that exceeds the cost of having to do them.

Progress Meetings (or Monitoring Meetings)

If you are lucky, and your team is nearby for most of the time, you can call progress meetings on a regular or even a spontaneous basis. If you are not in this situation, you will have to find other ways of having meetings (such as, perhaps, "virtual meetings" via the Internet or e-mail). Two things need to happen for progress meetings to work:

- The meetings themselves must happen (meetings often get pushed aside by more urgent problems), and

- Progress must be discussed at the meeting, even if progress is slow or problematic (if the problem is a sensitive one, discuss it sensitively rather than avoid it altogether).

Do not have so many progress meetings that they become irrelevant (i.e. not enough time has elapsed for any progress to be made). Try to arrange progress meetings to take place in roughly the same time-frame as major tasks need to be completed. Have the meetings regularly but don't feel that you must never comment on progress unless you are at a progress meeting.

Progress Reports (Process Documentation)

Traditional project management is well-known for its reliance on documentation. It is our view that documentation for its own sake is a waste of time — if the documents are not needed or are not read, why go on producing them? However, do remember that the onus is on you to keep your stakeholders informed so, if stakeholders are not reading the documents, another way must be found to keep them up-to-date on progress. It is often easier to keep stakeholders informed by having face-to-face meetings or telephone conversations with them. This can be more efficient and can help to build good relationships.

If this change project is to serve as a template for future changes within your organisations, keep a "project log" rather than attempting to formally document everything. A log is better because it allows for comment on *how* things happened/were managed as well as what happened/was managed.

Steering Committee

A common occurrence in large change projects, or projects which are complex (for example, have a number of funders who have no experience of working together) is to have a steering committee whose purpose is to provide guidance if or when the project encounters difficulties. Steering committees are usually made up of representatives of key stakeholders, including clients, and are particularly useful when tough decisions have to be made such as major trade-offs between time, cost and quality.

Steering committees are, frequently, "political". That is, they are often constructed as a forum for decision-making, particularly when the manager suspects that there may be a lack of trust between the stakeholders or when different stakeholders have different (but legitimate) views about the change. You can seek to confine any arguments or difficulties to the steering committee rather than have such problems affect your team.

In the case of progress meetings, progress reports and steering committees, the emphasis should be on deviations and variations from the plan. You must be able to give as much information as possible on the cause of any variation, the implications of the variation, and, if the problem has already been solved, what steps were taken to do so. If the problem is being referred to senior management or the steering committee, you should also outline the options available for limiting the consequences of the variation on the achievement of your overall objectives for this change project.

CONTROLLING ALTERATIONS TO THE PLAN

As noted, most of the effort that will be spent on monitoring and controlling will focus on deviations, variations, and alterations to your plan. Such alterations are almost inevitable in change projects — plans rarely fully reflect real life. In many cases, the alterations are "caused" not by real life, but by some keen team member wanting to add extra dimensions to the quality or functionality of the overall change. For example, a young geologist looking for natural gas discovers that, if they drilled just ten metres further down, they could test for other minerals too. This extra ten metres could add 5 per cent to the cost of the project, however, and even delay it, so the manager has to make a decision quickly about such suggested alterations to the scope and plan of the project.

One simple way of seeking to control these alterations (although it can be time-consuming) is to have a procedure for approving all alterations (or, at least, all which will have an adverse effect on the critical path). This can certainly help reduce the number of "WIBNIs" (i.e. "wouldn't it be nice if"-kinds of alterations, such as the one the geologist was thinking of above) and, in the case of client-proposed alterations, it can help you to renegotiate the scope and to secure the client's commitment to provide further resources, if necessary.

The most common procedure for controlling alterations to the plan is to have Request-for-Alteration Forms which can be kept simple but should contain the following types of information:

- A brief description of the alteration

- The reason for the alteration — what benefits will it bring to the client, organisation or to the overall impact of the change?

- An estimate of the impact of the alteration on other tasks or phases of the change project

- An estimate of the cost of the alteration

- Suggestions as to who will actually do any additional work required to effect the alteration or by the alteration itself.

You, the manager (with, perhaps, the steering committee, if there is one) are ultimately responsible for making the decision as it is you who is best placed to see the overall impact of any alterations on the budget, quality and deadline for the change (and, of course, it is you who will be responsible).

Finally, two further points about change control procedures such as these request-for-alteration forms:

1. These procedures should be agreed and established before the change project gets underway, and

2. For them to be seen as useful, they must prompt quicker and fairer decisions than not having procedures at all.

Extract from Interview —
Manager, EU Programme for Training Arts Sector
Business Managers

"With a training programme of such long duration and so many stakeholders, it must have been difficult to keep the whole thing on track?"

"Yes, I had to try to meet the expectations of both the EU and the trainees. One advantage was that the time scale and end-products of different parts of the programme were defined in very specific terms so, once we made the agreement on the specification for the programme, we knew what had to be controlled and we had a way of doing it."

"But surely some deviations crept in?"

"Well, the issue of the trainees' business plans gave me a lot of grief. Part of the original terms of reference for the programme was a requirement that, before they got their qualification, every trainee had to produce a business plan to a certain specification. The production of these plans was also a standard for us in so far as we wouldn't receive the final instalment of the funding until this requirement was fulfilled. So I started off with the assumption that this standard had to be met: for me, it was part of the quality of the final outcome. At first, the trainees seemed to share my view and most of them were willing to put in the effort to make their plan. But some resisted, one guy in particular who began to argue with me about having to do it. He regarded the plan as a pointless exercise, wasting time that he could have been spending on actually launching his product portfolio. He insisted that the programme was meant to help him to achieve his goals and that any use of his time should fit in with his priorities as an entrepreneur."

"So this was one individual who wanted you to adjust the standard, loosen it up in his case?"

"A particularly vocal individual, too. He was arguing that the output, the completed plan, had little meaning as an indicator of the achievement of the intended objective which was the establishment of a viable business. The discussion set me thinking about a broader standard underlying my own role — a real, though implicit, one which was to meet the participants' needs. There was also a veiled message in there, since the interim evaluation of the whole programme was going on at that point. This evaluation was going to carry real weight as the participants themselves were heavily involved in the assessment. At first, I was inclined to adjust our standard in his case, and simply let him off making a business plan. I could have rationalised it as a necessity to respond to the emerging needs of each individual — they were adults, after all, and could take responsibility for themselves."

"But then . . . ?"

"But then, as you've guessed, I decided there were really no grounds for waiving the requirement in his case, given that he had known about it when he joined the programme. I was taking into account both principle (I sought to apply the rules with fairness and transparency to the whole group) and practicality (I might need leeway to re-negotiate other standards at a later stage). As the discussion dragged out, it worried me because I couldn't afford to jeopardise the time dimensions which would also have pushed up the cost."

"So, what about this discontented trainee?"

"Luckily, the administrator had a very good rapport with him and she was able to listen and empathise with how he felt, on a personal level. So, though I didn't shift the standard, he felt that his views were given a hearing. The administrator also put the question in a wider perspective, suggesting that knowing how to put together a business plan might come in useful later in his career."

"And did it, do you know?"

"Well, if it did, we never heard. However, this episode had two good effects: I discovered that, if need be, I could exercise tight control by playing the bad cop and leave the good cop role to the administrator. And the other one was the way it actually allowed me to deliver on the broader standard, of responding to ongoing needs and areas of concern, through a looser kind of control. It alerted me to the value of having eyes and ears out in the system."

"What do you mean?"

"Well, as a manager, I was at a remove, but the administrator was on the ground and she had high visibility and high trust among the trainees. So she was very tuned in to the day-to-day stuff, informally monitoring how people were getting on, the quality of the functioning of the whole programme. So, at least I could be taking a helicopter view most of the time, but I was able to home in on a specific area if, say, mediation was needed. So the control was very active, with lots of two-way communication."

"You mentioned the benefit of having some leeway to re-negotiate standards if required. What did this mean?"

"Well, with the transnational partners, a difference of views emerged. They wanted to emphasise and develop the accreditation aspect of the programme. We weren't convinced of how the benefits of offering accreditation would outweigh the demands and costs of it. So, for our part, we opted to follow our trainees' preferences. They showed great appreciation of the hands-on practical characteristics of the programme and accreditation didn't rate very highly with them."

"How did that work out?"

"On that, we explained our reservations to the transnational partners and, after lots of tense discussion, agreed to go our separate ways about the accreditation arrangements. We felt, and our trainees felt, that that particular output was not essential to success of the programme."

"What about controlling the other dimensions of performance?"

"Well, I was really proud of how small a variance we showed on the cost. It was absolutely infinitesimal — not even 10p in over half a million pounds."

"How did you manage it?"

"It resulted from keeping a really close and steady watch on the cash flow and cumulative expenditure throughout the whole programme. We knew that the EU, the funders, would take a real interest in this aspect and that, if there was a significant discrepancy at the end, they would possibly audit the books for the whole thing. So we kept in close contact with them on this and negotiated permission to shift money from one budget category to another on one or two occasions."

"Well done, and many thanks."

Chapter 8

MANAGING PEOPLE THROUGH THE CHANGE: AN INTRODUCTION

INTRODUCTION

We are about to make a radical shift in focus away from the "getting the job done" side of change management to the "looking after the people" side. The first half of this book, the "getting the job done" side, followed a chronological sequence according to the different phases of the planning and control of change projects. The second half, the half that we're about to begin, does not have such a linear sequence as it focuses on the different "soft" aspects of management practice that you will be putting in place throughout the change or which you will use at specific times only, times which cannot always be scheduled. Of course, a focus on both the job and on the people side is necessary in management. Looking after your people is a means to ensuring that the job gets done as it is the people who will make change happen.

The people side of "old" or traditional project management was, in the early stages of its evolution, often ignored. Many of the early textbooks are completely devoid of references to people management (except for chapters on "resource allocation"). This is not all that surprising when we remember that much of the discipline of "old" project management was born in the highly command-oriented environment of the US military. Military bosses did not have to worry too much about their people management skills as they had rank and authority on their side. Command-and-control has lost much of its appeal as an approach to managing people and, consequently, managers have had to develop other ways of motivating, influencing and controlling the performance of their human resources (people).

All managers have a preferred management style, that is, a way of looking at things, of solving problems, of achieving their goals and working with colleagues. This style is important because its impact is felt by the manager him or herself and by those who work with the manager. For you, a key aspect of your success will be understanding how you affect those around you and your staff in particular.

MANAGEMENT STYLES

One common way of categorising management style is to see managers as being primarily *task-oriented* (their main concern is getting the job done) or as being primarily *people-oriented* (concerned with ensuring people work well together). In particular, the management of change is often a messy business and rationality and logic are not enough. People's behaviour is driven by a variety of factors, including rationality, but also emotion, habit, politics (hidden or unconscious agendas) and the need for approval and affection. Managing people well means accepting that they (and you) are multi-dimensional.

It is interesting to note that most early change project managers were primarily task-oriented. However, research into a spate of project "failures" in the 1970s and 1980s led to the conclusion that managers who were lacking in people management skills were significantly more likely to run into major difficulties than those who were proficient in people management. This was because it was factors such as lack of communication, co-operation and co-ordination, poor teamwork, friction in the team, and lack of consultation that were most frequently implicated in these failed change projects.

In this book, we have deliberately structured the contents to reflect both a task- and a people-orientation. This is because at times during the life of a project, you may need to be task-oriented and, at other times, a people-orientation will be required. You will have to make judgements about which orientation is appropriate.

The purpose of this chapter, and of the following ones, is to help you in your judgement on these matters.

When we think about managing resources, our ideas about the appropriate way to achieve this may vary according to which resource we have in mind. For instance, when we think about managing money, we may concern ourselves with its security (how to make sure it is not misappropriated) and, usually, with its investment (how to make sure it at least maintains its value over time). When we think about managing time, other concerns may emerge, such as getting the best value from it (it can't be "banked" and will elapse whether we use it well or squander it). Information is another resource and our concerns with managing information frequently centre on how to ensure it is easily accessible, relevant, up-to-date, etc. All of these are facets of management style but it is attitude to people which is usually the most telling characteristic.

Management style is often characterised by whether you see human resources, like money, as a cost or an investment. Like time, are human resources something to be planned, controlled and finite (a very western perspective!)? Or are human resources something which can be seen as having a much longer horizon and which are capable of expansion and/or contraction according to the particular circumstances of a given event? Figure 8.1 illustrates some of the polarities of managerial attitudes to human resources.

As you can imagine, managers who are primarily on the left-hand side of these polarities will have a management style which is open, growth-oriented, proactive and concerned with adding value to their human resources. We can summarise this style as developmental (i.e. capable of seeing opportunities and of nurturing them to fruition). Managers to the right of these polarities, on the other hand, will be controlling, saving-oriented, reactive and concerned with getting as much as they can from people. This style can be summarised as conservative.

Figure 8.1: Some Management Style Polarities

Of course, both develop and conserve styles have certain elements which may recommend them as approaches to people management. Equally, neither style is perfect. The ideal solution would be that each manager would choose that style which best matches the circumstances of the particular change on which they are working. For instance, if your senior manager stipulated that you had to employ three new trainees on a change project that really only required one junior, you might be justified in seeing the surplus two as something of an unwanted cost (at least in the short term). You might be worried that the development of these surplus people might soak up an inordinate amount of your time or of your training budget. You might then attempt to "cut your losses" by scheduling the extra trainees to do just routine low-level work, requiring little skills or supervision, so that you can concentrate on developing the skills and capacity of your other team members. In this way, you could be both developmental (in relation to the wanted people) and conservative (in relation to the surplus people).

It might seem as if the philosophy of "old" project management would suggest that a conservative management style would be most appropriate for change project managers. Certainly, this was the assumption for a long time. However, more recent experience in change management suggests that managers are often most successful by being *fixed* in relation to getting the job done but by being *flexible* in relation to managing people. In other words, once the objectives and scope have been agreed, the manager should concentrate on reaching these agreed objectives (by planning, controlling, etc.). However, given that plans are, in effect, attempts to predict the future, it is only by being flexible and proactive in relation to people that a manager is likely to achieve the objectives of the change.

Thus, if there is one ideal management style it could be summarised as being both task- and people-oriented, and as being conservative (in relation to the task) and as being developmental (in relation to the people).

Figure 8.2: The Ideal Change Project Management Style

	Task Management	People Management
Developmental		✓
Conservative	✓	

MANAGING (HUMAN) RESOURCES

One of the most useful ways of looking at resource management (including human resource management) is to use the input-output-outcome model that we used in the last chapter. This model, put simply, says that we must add value to inputs to convert them to outputs, and these outputs in turn should lead to our intended outcome. To take a basic business example, we should add value to our raw materials (inputs) by converting or processing them to products for sale (outputs) in order that we make a profit (intended outcome). This model, though somewhat theoretical, represents the fundamentals of all management, including people management.

If we take our input to be people, then, according to this model, the processing should change them in some way so that they meet our output specification, which, in turn, should help us meet our desired outcome. In simple English, we should aim to manage people (input) so that we both achieve the project objective and add value to our resources in the process (output). This should ensure that we satisfy our clients and our staff (outcome). A closer look at these different components makes the implications for change managers clearer.

Table 8.1: Managing to Achieve Objectives and Add Value to People

	Description	Manager Interest
Input	People — a "bundle" of knowledge, skills and attitudes, all of which may require managing.	What kind of people are required by this project? What criteria should be used to select the team?
Processing or Conversion	The processes, systems and structures within/ through/by which people have to work. Do these processes add or subtract value from the inputs?	How to make it easy for a person to contribute to the change team? How is the team structured? What are the channels of communication? How does a team member develop new skills or get help? How are team members motivated?
Output or Deliverable	What should be the end product of processing these inputs (people) in these ways?	How can team members contribute to the achievement of the objective of the change (main output)? How can the value of a team member be increased (secondary output)?
Outcome	The result of producing the above output (achieving objectives); adding value to the people on the way.	How to satisfy clients (both commissioning and end clients) and ensure job satisfaction for team members.

One way of summarising the above table is to think of a "virtuous circle" whereby the more you can add value to your people during the project, the more value your people can add to the project.

Figure 8.3: "Virtuous Cycle" of Added Value

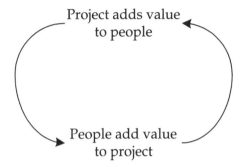

KEY PEOPLE MANAGEMENT SKILLS

The questions raised by looking at the above diagram and table may have already provided you with some insight into the sorts of skills that are considered to be critical for effective people management.

Some of the skills implicit in Table 8.1 on the previous page include:

- Teamwork — knowing what criteria to use to choose a team that will meet the project requirements and will work well together

- Motivating — how to keep people interested and contributing

- Delegation — one of the most frequently used forms of staff development.

In addition to these skills are the two basic skills or building blocks of managing people, i.e. *communicating* and *influencing*. In fact, these latter two skills underpin most other management skills and, on their own, have been said to account for 80 per cent of people management success.

So far, we have been concentrating on the people who are internal to the change project. However, as we know, managers also have to manage external stakeholders, such as clients, suppliers, financiers/funders and others. Managing people who are external to the project will require some of the above-mentioned skills (in particular, communicating and influencing). In addition, a further people management skill which is very useful to change managers is the skill of *negotiating*. Negotiation is a constant feature of management, from the objective-setting phase through to signing off.

Finally, two other skills are often needed for successful people management. These last two are "rainy day" skills, that is, skills which are only required when things are going badly but which, like an umbrella, are the best thing around if heavy rain or a storm is forecast. If the storm is internal, the skill of *managing conflict* might be the most effective umbrella. If the storm is external, the skills of *consultancy* might be very useful. Both managing conflict and consultancy skills are based on the earlier key skills of communication and influencing and, often, include some of the elements of negotiation too.

These are the main people skills which make for a good change manager. However, as mentioned earlier, the ideal management style involves getting the right balance between a task- and a people-orientation. One way you can do more of this is by deliberately trying to bring a people-orientation to the task side of the job. For example, often the best way to set objectives, to plan, estimate and schedule, is to involve stakeholders in the process rather than simply to inform them of the results of the process. This involvement not only makes sense in terms of adding value to the people involved but also ensures that you are more likely to get the job done to everyone's satisfaction. Simple techniques to involve people include brainstorming, workshops and, of course, the skills of communication and consultation which we have already mentioned.

Extract from Interview —
Change Manager, Private Hospital
(Introduction of New Day-Care Unit)

"OK, I'd like to ask you a more general question about you as a manager. What would you say was your management style?"

"I think I would tend to adopt the style very much that you tell people at the outset what's expected of them; where possible, I'd get their agreement that these are reasonable expectations. If somebody doesn't agree with those expectations, I think, in certain circumstances, like when you're working to a fixed deadline or you're under pressure, I'd tend to stick to these expectations and say 'well, that's the job'. In other words, in a lot of cases, the expectations are set by the nature of what you're trying to do — inevitably, you have deadlines and targets and these aren't always negotiable so you don't always have the option of bending the rules to accommodate everybody."

"Would these expectations include qualitative dimensions like attitude and, if so, how would you measure them?"

"Absolutely, say, in relation to patients, or customers as they're often called now, it'd be by direct observation of what the staff were doing and also using patient feedback forms but these aren't ideal because you usually just get complaints and you need the whole picture. But, back to management style, yes, letting people know your expectations includes how you want them to behave towards patients/customers and giving them regular feedback and discussing their performance. How you deal with poor performance depends on the individual you're dealing with: some respond to pressure, some need help. I think it's important to have some structure to the feedback, for instance, giving a written report pointing out the areas of good and bad, asking them to respond, setting goals for improvement and using disciplinary sanctions if necessary. If they need help, you're often trying to weigh up the consequences of their poor performance in maybe one area against possibly losing them altogether for a while, say if they have to go off for training or end up getting sick."

"How would your staff describe your style?"

"Most of them would have said that it was more demanding working for me than in other parts of the health service but that's because they came from areas where there were lower standards for quality performance.

I think they would also say I was fair — everyone knew where they stood from day one and they disputed my expectations when they were too high. I expect people to expect high standards from me and I expect them of the people that I work with too. I suppose, in general, there'll always be people who like you more than others and people you like more than others, but, even so, I tried to treat all of them with respect and equality, regardless of whether I liked them better or knew them from before. I did my best to treat them the same, no favours."

"What about when there were problems or when one of your team was unsure of what to do next? What happened in these kinds of cases?"

"Well, as part of the training before the opening of the Unit, we put together a kind of manual, literally step-by-step from a patient being admitted for treatment through to their discharge from the Unit. We thought it would be good to have a reference in times of problems and a standardised way of dealing with the processing because some of the people were inexperienced. I was off-site a good bit so the manual meant people could help themselves to a good extent. But there were times when problems came up, especially with operational things like appointment systems and medical records, so we noted all of these kinds of problems and designed solutions to them and there was ongoing training too. Often, they'd come to me with one of these problems and I'd sit down with them for half-an-hour or so and go through it with them and we'd work it out, clarify the necessary points and so on."

"What would happen when, say, a GP or referring consultant complained about an aspect of how the Unit was doing?"

"The most common complaint we'd get from doctors whose patients were due for treatment or in for treatment related to bottlenecks and waiting lists, and we'd have to locate the problem, sort it out, see what was going on, and, if it was caused by staff, give them more help, more training, even add a bit of 'motivation' (a threat, if necessary!). But morale in the Unit was good, everyone was excited about it, they were ambitious and came to work here because they wanted to, because they saw it as a step above what they had been doing and as the way that hospital services were going and they wanted to get in at the beginning. They wanted a challenge."

"Was everybody good, then, at their job?"

"Well, inevitably, there were times when people weren't performing up to what I considered was a reasonable level. But usually it came down to a training issue: they didn't know what to do or, in one case, they misunderstood something they'd been trained in already and were carrying out a procedure in the wrong way. This didn't cause a problem at that point in the process but it did two steps further down. The problem kept recurring in the regular quality audits that I was doing and none of us realised what was causing it. I had to sit down with them for a day, watch what they were doing and eventually it became obvious what it was, we tracked it down, by going back to stage one and monitoring and reviewing every stage of the process and checking the outputs at every stage."

"Was everyone involved in this problem-solving?"

"Yeah, but generally problems came to me, were handed to me mostly even by the experienced people in the early days. For the first six months or so after the Unit opened, all problems came directly to me which I actually encouraged because I saw that problems were a good way of testing the system and training people, solving them together with the person or alongside me while I was solving it. It often involved phoning IT or building maintenance and they preferred me to do that but I would always make sure the person who brought the problem to me saw how I solved it and I'd try to make sure that they could do it next time if needed. I tended to get more problems from one or two individuals than from the others — people have different levels of initiative and comfort and some took more of my time than others. But, that's part of the job — you need them working with you and you have to start from where they're at."

Chapter 9

COMMUNICATING AND NEGOTIATING

INTRODUCTION

Communication is the bedrock of good people management. In a sense, it is one of the most fundamental management skills and, often, the one that is most taken for granted. Effective communicators possess a number of skills of which the most critical is self-knowledge.

Communication is strange in that it takes place whenever two (or more) people are together and, in addition, much of it is unintentional. Communication is not just about what we say, it is about who we are, what we think, and how we convey our thoughts. In a sense, this is the Zen of communication!

Communication is, of course, a key aspect of negotiation too. But negotiation is more than just communication, it is a way of resolving conflict. Negotiation is something that all managers are required to do, in many cases over quite routine "conflicts" such as requests from staff for time off.

In change management, communication and negotiation are especially useful because of the "pressure-cooker" environment which strict time–cost–quality specifications can induce. Such constraints and tight control over resources in general are often the very thing which make effective communication and negotiation more difficult yet more necessary.

UNDERSTANDING COMMUNICATION

Communication can be both very simple and very complex. It is something that each of us has been doing since we were born. You would not hold your current position if you did not already know how to communicate. Therefore, this chapter is not about the skills of communication *per se* (such as speaking, listening, writing, etc.) but concentrates more on how to improve communication through understanding how it can go wrong.

Below is a simplified diagram of communication. It shows that communication, not surprisingly, involves the sending and receiving of messages. The diagram simplifies all communication, whether by mechanical means, such as radio, or by more personal means, such as face-to-face conversation. It also shows that there are six places where problems can arise in communication.

Figure 9.1: A Simple Model of Communication

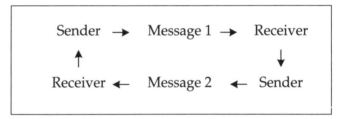

Some of the more common problems include:

1. The message made sense to the sender, but not to the receiver — it was phrased ("encoded") in the sender's jargon or assumed an unreasonable level of understanding or knowledge of the receiver.

2. The language in the message was ambiguous so that the receiver interpreted ("decoded") it in a way that was not what the sender had intended.

3. The message was sent at a time that was convenient for the sender but inconvenient for the receiver — for instance, the receiver may have been trying to do several things at the same time as the message arrived.

4. The message was not complete — for example, it was not clear what was required of the receiver.

5. The message was inherently conflicting — a simple example is when the verbal language and the body language are not congruent as in a sender saying "I don't care" but looking very upset.

6. The message was met with silence — silence is itself, of course, a powerful message and should tell the sender that something may have gone wrong.

It follows, then, that there are a number of factors which need to be right for communication to be easy and to be effective.

The most obvious starting point is the *message* itself. It must be phrased in a way that makes it clear and understandable to the receiver. (If you don't know who the receiver is going to be, a common rule-of-thumb, again, developed by the US army but widely applicable to other settings, says that you should assume that the receiver is an intelligent fifteen-year-old and use language that a fifteen-year-old could be expected to understand.) Another way of checking the usefulness of a message is to use the "ACAI" test (**A**ttention–**C**omprehension–**A**cceptance–**I**mplementation): will the message gain the receiver's attention, will the receiver understand it, will they accept it, and will they act on it? If there is doubt in your mind about any of these four aspects, you may want to re-think your message or how you are choosing to convey it.

The other side of the communication is, of course, the *human side*. You won't be surprised to learn that this is often the more problematic side.

When we communicate, we communicate more than the message. We also communicate our view of our relationship with the other person. In addition, this relationship is usually ongoing: it has a past and, usually, a future. The messages that are sent and received will be interpreted in the context of these factors. For example, let us take a scenario where there have been problems between a manager and one of her staff over the quality of the work of that staff member. One day the manager asks the staff member to "drop in to see her". Let us suppose that the staff member is less than happy about this request. In these circumstances, it is possible that the following "latent messages" can also be read into the communication:

- An assumption on the manager's part that the request will be respected because of the power relationship between them (of course, it may not)

- An assumption that the staff member's other work is less important than a meeting with the manager

- An assumption that the (intended) purpose of the meeting will be to convey an unpleasant message

- An assumption that other members of staff will see him going into the manager's office and will wonder what's going on

- An assumption that the staff member will be asked to address the issue of the quality of his work.

You can imagine that the effects of these assumptions on the part of the staff member will be to heighten his anxiety. If he is anxious, he will probably be a less effective communicator. The manager may also be anxious: managers rarely relish having to confront their staff about their work.

These sorts of assumptions can take place every day in every place of work. The people in this scenario are not unusual, nor are they paranoid. This simple scenario points to the numerous factors in a communication event which are important to the success of that event, not the least of which is emotion or a state such as anxiety.

FIVE FACTORS IN COMMUNICATION

Below are some of the main factors which play a major part in communication.

1. **Process**. Communication is a process, not a series of unrelated events. Communication is cumulative: messages are sent and received in the context of this ongoing developing process. In addition, we cannot "undo" a communication (whether the message is spoken or silent) — if it has been problematic, it is likely that more (active) communication will be needed to resolve the problem.

2. **Relationship**. A key question for communicators is the relationship between themselves and their "audience" — how do they want this relationship to be after the communication? If they do not want to unnecessarily damage this relationship, care must be taken not to intentionally or unintentionally convey a distorted or inappropriate interpretation of the relationship as the distortion is, very often, what the receiver will attend to, rather than the message.

3. **Emotion**. We are emotional beings and we remain so even in the so-called rational environment of work. Emotions colour our communications. If we are highly emotional, we may find it difficult to communicate effectively. On the other hand, a complete denial of emotion may also impact adversely on our communication. The point here is that we generally (although often unintentionally) communicate our emotions in our body language (our stance, our voice, our facial expressions, etc.). However, if our emotions are a barrier to getting results, they usually need to be made explicit. It is worth noting too that emotions need to be met with empathy, not rationality. You cannot reason away an emotion.

4. **Noise**. In this case, noise refers not only to physical noise which may literally prevent us from hearing the message, but also to "psychological" noise which may have the same effect. Psychological noise is often the result of stress (acute and/or chronic) or of emotion, as mentioned above. If your messages don't seem to be getting through, check for noise.

5. **Self-perception and our perception of others**. When we communicate, whether verbally or by our body language, we inevitably communicate something about ourselves. This is what accounts for the "first impressions" syndrome. We are able to read something about everyone from the way they look, talk, act, etc., as well as by what they say. Knowing how we feel about ourselves and how we feel about the people with whom we are communicating is a major advantage in clearing the lines for our messages. If we feel nervous in the presence of a certain person, we are likely to communicate some of that nervousness. If we feel negative about the person to whom we are talking, again, we are likely to communicate some of this. The main point here is that the better we know what we are thinking about ourselves and about our receivers, the more effective will be our communication. This is because we will be more alert to the possibility of misinterpretation and we will be more sensitive to the need for constant checking.

Effective communication is a two-way process. As the diagram earlier suggests, there needs to be a loop back from the receiver to the original sender to show that the message has been received and understood (or, if misunderstood, to allow the sender to amend it and re-send it). Although the receiver plays a part, the primary onus is on the sender to check that the message has been received.

This checking means taking all of the above factors into account. If the message is to pass the ACAI test, the sender must check for assumptions which may be inaccurate, and the sender must also check for emotion and for noise. If the sender wants the message understood and acted upon, the sender must do most of the work of communication. However, if you find yourself on the receiving end of poor communication, and it is in your interest to clarify that communication, checking back to the sender is also a very useful way of ensuring the integrity of a message.

NEGOTIATION

Negotiation is one of the most common ways of trying to resolve a conflict of interests (other approaches to handling interpersonal conflict will be covered in Chapter 13). When we think of negotiation, we often think of compromise, of each party conceding a little of their interests for the sake of getting a concession on their most important interests. Reflecting back to the five factors in communication which were mentioned above, it is easy to see why good communication awareness is a key component of effective negotiation.

Change managers can benefit from good negotiation skills throughout the course of their change project, for example, when:

- **Initiating the change**. Negotiation with commissioning clients on aspects of the time–cost–quality specification or on the objectives of the change; negotiation with end users — e.g. a particular community or population group which is to benefit from the change — about their expectations of the outcome

- **Dealing with stakeholders**. Negotiation with other stakeholders on the same issues or for resources — e.g. you might have to negotiate with the Personnel Department for the release from other work of key people for your team

- **Managing the team**. Negotiation with your team or with individual members of it about the Work Breakdown Structure and about their roles and the estimates for the time they reckon they will need to complete different tasks

- **Implementing the change**. Negotiation with all stakeholders (internal and external) in the event of any deviation from the time-cost-quality specification — e.g. missing the deadlines for critical tasks, budget overruns, changes to the design, etc.

When you add in the routine negotiation that managers engage in with their staff over such issues as time off, annual leave, requests for amendments to work done, etc., you can see that negotiation is an activity that you may find yourself doing all of the time — in fact, it could be said that anyone who operates within resource constraints will be a negotiator.

SUBSTANTIVE ISSUES AND RELATIONSHIP ISSUES

One of the key distinctions that an effective negotiator needs to make before entering into negotiations is the distinction between the *substantive* issue (what resources are being sought?) and the *relationship* issue (how do I want our relationship to be after the negotiation is over?). This dichotomy is similar to the one we mentioned earlier regarding management style, i.e. between a task orientation and a people orientation.

Making this distinction can help to overcome some of the difficulties that can be associated with poor communication (remember the five factors?). If the negotiators are clear about what they are looking for and about how they want their relationship to be, they are much less likely to communicate inadvertent, inaccurate or inappropriate messages to the other side during their negotiation.

In relation to the substantive issue, if possible, be clear in your own mind about what your *optimal* solution would look like and about what your *minimal acceptable* solution would be. For example, imagine you were negotiating with a senior manager from another department in your organisation for the release of a key person, someone whose expertise is critical to the successful implementation of your change. You know that you will need this person in four weeks' time, at the latest. However, you also know that, if she could be released earlier, you could actually start early on one of the critical tasks of your project and, therefore, relieve some of the pressure that you are expecting as you get closer to implementation. You also know that you cannot afford for her to arrive too early as your budget cannot stretch too far. Your minimal solution is for her to arrive on time but you also have an optimal solution which would probably be your opening stance in the negotiation.

There is often a great deal of debate about whether, in negotiation, you should "top up" your optimal solution (i.e. build in some slack) in case the other party only offers, for example, 90 per cent of your request. There is no one right answer to this question: it is a matter of judgement, of knowing the other party, and of one's own ethics.

With regard to the relationship issue, just as an optimal target is set for the substantive issue, so also should you set one for the relationship. Even though negotiation is a conflict resolution mechanism, it normally takes place within the context of an on-going relationship. Put bluntly, you will probably need or want to work again with the other party and, therefore, it is normally un-wise to risk irreparable damage to the relationship for the sake of winning on the substantive issue.

For this reason, it is worth thinking through how you want the relationship to be after the negotiation has ended. If you want it to remain good (or at least workable), you need to prepare your communication in advance.

SOME RULES FOR EFFECTIVE NEGOTIATION

There are a few "golden rules" which, if followed, can signifi-cantly improve the likelihood of resolving a conflict of interests through negotiation. (These rules are based on the work of Fisher and Ury in their best-selling guide to negotiating *Getting to Yes*.) Of course, the question of whether to adopt them or not is a mat-ter of personal judgement.

An Ethical Approach to Negotiation

Negotiation, as we have said, is a way of trying to resolve a con-flict of interest, usually over a resource issue. However, this does not necessarily mean that one party has to win or that compro-mise is the only jointly acceptable solution. Parties choose to ne-gotiate in order to win what they are seeking. It follows, therefore, that the optimal solution for both parties is win-win (i.e. both parties win). This may sound like an impossibility, but it does not have to be. However, for a win-win solution to emerge, both sides have to be willing and able to:

- Focus on the objective of what they are trying to achieve (in relation to both the substantive and the relationship issue), not on the means, or on the positions or roles that they play

- Be creative and inventive and problem-solve together in order to find a solution which allows them both to achieve their preferred outcome

- Be tough on the problem but gentle on the people.

In practice, it should be acknowledged that these may be difficult to achieve. To look at what they mean in a "real-life" scenario, let's look at the problem mentioned before, that of the manager trying to secure (from a divisional manager somewhere else in the organisation) the timely appointment of a key person to his change management team.

Focus on Outcomes

The outcome that the change manager is seeking is to implement the change on time. The appointment of the key person is a means to this end. If the manager goes into the negotiation focusing exclusively on the appointment, the options for achieving his outcome are much more limited.

The divisional manager is also looking for an outcome, as yet not fully known, but likely to centre on not jeopardising his own work plans through the untimely loss of a key person. The change manager would be wise to check on what risks are perceived by the divisional manager in the loss of that person.

If these two parties focus solely on their positions (especially given that the divisional manager is likely to have more formal authority in this situation) or roles, they are much more likely to end up in a power struggle which will militate against them being able to achieve a win-win result.

Problem-solve Together

Here, we need to imagine the two managers sitting down together, being open about the risks that are potentially in the offing for each of them in the appointment of the person (especially re-garding the timing of the appointment) and making sure that each knows what the other is trying to achieve (i.e. on-time implementation of the change and, in the case of the divisional manager, minimal disruption to the achievement of his divisional objectives). They then need to consider what options might be available to them to secure a mutually agreeable outcome.

Several options are mentioned and, in the end, the two parties agree to the following win-win solution: the divisional manager agrees to the early release of the key person as he recognises that his division's sales will suffer at least as much as anyone else if the change project is not implemented on time and successfully. He also agrees to keep this person on his payroll up for an extra two weeks, even though the person will be working on the change, in return for early informal feedback on how the change is going as this early information will give him maximum time to adjust his new market sales plan. Both parties are happy with this outcome as the company needs both the change and an increase in sales to new markets.

Be Tough on the Problem, Not on the People

Let's imagine that someone in the manager's team hears that the negotiations will soon be taking place and advises the manager to be careful in his dealings with the divisional chief as he has been known before to change his mind when it suited him.

The manager might wish to explore this in the negotiations. He is conscious of the fact that he doesn't want to annoy the divisional chief so he goes with the rule of being tough on the problem but gentle on the people. He does this by being explicit in *describing the problem* ("I understand that, in the past, circumstances have meant that you have had to change your stance on agreements made about the transfer of staff..."), *not on labelling the person* ("I hear, through the grapevine, that you have not always honoured your agreement about releasing staff — is this going to be the case here?"). Describing the problem is a much more fruitful avenue to resolving the problem. Labelling the person in a tough way (in the above example, implying that he is dishonourable as opposed to allowing him save face by reference to larger "circumstances") will not help communication and this, in turn, will make it more difficult for the two sides to explore the problem and find a solution. It will also make trust more difficult to establish which will make any project much harder to manage.

Tips for Improving Communication during Negotiation

- **Flag your messages (except when you want to disagree)**: flagging is a way of getting the attention of the other party to what you are about to say, propose, suggest, etc. For example, *"I'd like to make a proposal"* and *"Can I ask you about that?"* are common flags.

- **Listen and reflect back**: put energy into listening and demonstrate your listening by reflecting back to the speaker what you think were the main points of their message. Active listening is one of the best ways of helping to establish trust.

- **Disclose feelings and emotions, don't act them**: if you are feeling fearful or concerned or frustrated, say so explicitly. Naming your emotion will help the other party to take account of it and to help you to deal with it. This also helps the other party to disclose any feelings or concerns that they may have about what is under discussion. It is better that you hear any concerns they may have while you're still "around the table" rather than later.

- **Avoid counter-proposals**: it is extremely difficult to build a good working relationship when one side's proposals for a resolution of the issue are simply met with the other side's proposals. In this way, there is very little listening or debate about the merits of the different proposals. Good ideas may be missed, trust takes longer to establish, and things may degenerate into a power play to establish who can shout (their proposal) loudest.

- **Avoid aggression and intimidation**: if you are feeling angry, say so. Macho tactics such as table-banging, threats to walk out on the discussion, shouting, etc. are obvious enemies to good communication and are usually just met with counter-attacking or defensive ploys. These will not help resolve conflict. The only time such tactics are "useful" is when the solution is already agreed or beyond the control/authority of the negotiators but, nonetheless, the negotiators have to be seen to have argued as strenuously as possible.

Finally, a useful personal performance measure is to rate yourself on a simple scale (say, out of ten) on your achievement of the substantive objective and again on the achievement of your relationship objective. If you are less than satisfied with your performance, seek feedback from someone you trust. For the feedback to be useful, ask for it to be very specific and focused on behaviour (e.g. what exactly did I do or say that made you think I was annoyed at that point?).

Extract from Interview — Project Manager, Construction Projects

"How are things going in the building business these days?"

"Well, I'm certainly not short of work as a project manager."

"But . . . ?"

"You're right, there's a 'but' and it's about giving clients the right message. For instance, a factory owner approached us recently. His waste recycling business was booming, and he wanted to build a new premises. For him it was a matter of putting up four walls and a roof to give him the square footage he needed for his staff and machinery."

"What was your response?"

"I tried to give him a balanced message. On the one hand we're delighted to take on the management of the project, but we can't just jump to the roof and four walls."

"That might confirm his worst fears about how complicated it all is . . ."

"Exactly, as he was new to the building business, we owed it to him to explain the whole process, and what he could achieve in quality terms, within his time and cost limits. So we had to keep clarifying his requirements, size, type and functionality of the new building, and negotiating with him about the ways we'd recommend him to proceed. You're really getting someone used to understanding and speaking an unfamiliar language."

"I suppose trust comes into it?"

"It does, very much. You're talking about a relationship, at times, holding his hand, because he had to take a gamble about the scheduling of the application for planning permission."

"Did you make a joint decision on that?"

"Well, since planning permission for phase one had gone through successfully, our credibility with the client was high. Phase two was more expensive. So, we discussed with him whether, concurrently with submitting the application, we should proceed to agree design and price. It would also be possible to sort out the technical issues. After a lot of listening and discussion, we established that for him the time considerations needed to take precedence. So that led to his agreement that we'd work concurrently. We each had to agree that it was a bit of a gamble. If our gamble had worked out, the doubling up on the scheduling would have put us on the right side of the costs, avoiding some of the impact of ever-rising building costs. He'd also have got away with less disruption to his business, which would also have saved him money."

"Can you say a bit more about the gamble?"

"We opted to spend substantial sums on progressing the project in advance of the grant of permission. We involved architects, contractors and quantity surveyors, as well as specialist consultants. Then we found that the project had gone to appeal, which left the client seriously exposed, financially speaking."

"How did he react?"

"He was very disappointed, especially as the first phase had gone through like a dream, but, by then, we had good channels of communication, and we had been keeping in close touch, so he wasn't taken totally by surprise. He was aware that there could be deviations from his original specification. As for us, we felt that we had behaved quite correctly. We gave him accurate information, and helped him think through the implications of the different options. As it happened, the increase in VAT that was announced after we had agreed the overall price was quite a sweetener, as it compensated us at least partly for extra expense that the delay caused."

Chapter 10

THE CHANGE TEAM

WHEN IS A TEAM A TEAM?

Most people have some experience of being in a team. Quite often, this experience is learned early in life in school. The structure of teams may vary from school to working life but, in general, the feeling of "teamness" is the same, regardless of age or of the purpose of the team. Equally, you may have been told that you were a member of a particular "team" but, for one reason or another, this so-called team was no more than a collection of people.

Before beginning to look at teamwork in detail, it is worth exploring what makes a team a team. When, for example, does a group of people become a team? When does a collection of individuals become a group? There are no absolute definitions of groups and teams but here are a number of common distinctions:

- A **collection of people** could be said to become a **group** when they have some *common purpose*, an awareness of their common purpose, and an *awareness of each other*. In addition, there must also be a collective *dependency* (on someone else) or *interdependency* and, finally, there must be *communication* between them. So, for example, a collection of individuals on the same bus may have the same common purpose (to travel to the terminus), they may be aware of each other and they are all dependent on a driver to get them there. However, they are not a group *per se* until they need to communicate to each other about their common purpose. This communication is most likely to happen if there is some threat to their goal (e.g. an accident or a bus strike).

- A **group** could be said to become a **team** when all of the above criteria are satisfied and, in addition, when their interdependency becomes more like *shared responsibility* for the working of the team and the achievement of objectives and when they spend a prolonged period of time together.

To summarise, a change project team can be said to exist when it:

- Has a common purpose (the achievement of the objectives)

- Demonstrates awareness of the individuals who comprise it

- Communicates, especially internally, about the achievement of its common purpose

- Has sufficient time together, and

- Is interdependent and mutually responsible for the achievement of its purpose and for the welfare of its members.

THREE DIMENSIONS OF TEAMWORK

In the last few decades, teamwork has become especially "trendy" because it can have several significant advantages over more traditional hierarchical organisational structures. Teams can be more flexible, more efficient, more creative, more responsive and more fun to work in than the alternative (the hierarchies). But, for teams to be like this, their leaders must also be different. You may remember when we discussed management styles, we distinguished between task-oriented and people-oriented managers and between developmental and conservative styles. Effective team management requires a balance between task- and people-orientation and, in general, a developmental rather than a conservative approach.

A common way to categorise this management style in relation to teamwork is to see the activity of team management as a trinity. You will need to actively manage all three and the way you manage each one will have knock-on effects on the others.

Figure 10.1: Three Dimensions of Teamwork

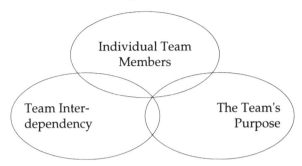

The three-sided approach to managing teams is useful because it serves to remind us that:

- Teams are set up to perform some *purpose* or achieve some particular set of results — teams are, almost by nature, goal-oriented and, for this reason, the goal must be "owned" by all of the team.

- Teams are made up of *individual team members*, each of whom must share the team's common goal but who will also have personal objectives which they want to satisfy through membership of the team (for example, one team member might want to impress the boss, another might be looking for skills enhancement, another might have a more social objective of wanting to work with another particular team member, etc.).

- Teams have a group dimension — they are *interdependent* and, for the team members to work collectively, structures and processes must evolve or be developed and they must be relatively durable.

The message from this is that teams, in general, need good leaders to be really effective. Depending on the nature of the change they have been created to implement, they will normally require *task specialists* (technical experts or professionals) but, regardless of the nature of the change, teams can greatly benefit from *process specialists* (people who are skilled in developing structured relationships and processes by which diverse individuals can work together in relative harmony). If you, as manager, are naturally more comfortable on the task-oriented side of management, you might want to ensure that your team is balanced by bringing in someone who is a people- or process-oriented person or by honing up your own people management skills.

THE PROCESS OF TEAMWORK

Imagine for a moment that you have been asked to manage a project which is concerned with teaching life skills (e.g. primary health care, domestic budgeting, etc.) to a group of young early school leavers in your locality. In addition, you have been told that you can write your own specification for the number and type of team members to help you implement this project and the locality has all types of specialists available within it who are willing to help (answers on a postcard, please, if you can identify this area!).

Your "dream team" probably includes several task specialists such as teachers, education experts, trainers, business advisors, etc. In addition, you might also have mentioned process specialists such as experienced youth workers (to help you understand "youth culture" and communicate with the end clients), people with leadership skills, people who are experienced team coaches and others who can help structure the team.

There is no hard-and-fast separation between task and process specialities — for instance, the youth workers in the above example could be thought of as both task and process specialists. In general, the sorts of teamwork activity which contribute to the *process* are relationship-building activities such as:

- Leading
- Guiding
- Co-ordinating
- Communicating (especially asking and listening)
- Supporting and encouraging
- Building trust and confidence

- Contributing new or different perspectives, and

- Resolving conflict, not ignoring or burying it.

If these kinds of relationship-building activities are absent, the team will not feel like a team and even the most important or urgent common purpose will not fully unite the individuals.

These process-oriented activities are normally, but not exclusively, the job of the manager. If you do not feel comfortable in doing these kinds of things, you should, as we have said before, try to find someone else in the team who is comfortable and skilled in building team relationships and, if necessary, deliberately recruit this kind of person. Alternatively, you can acquire the skills yourself through practice and feedback. If robust working relationships are not built between team members, there is a significant risk that the team will fall apart as soon as things get tough or tight (see Chapter 5 on estimating risk in projects).

As we said, relationship-building is not normally exclusive to the manager alone (it would be a full-time job for the manager if it were). The advice, therefore, is to recruit team members, where possible, who have experience of teamwork, who understand the interdependencies within teams, and who are good communicators and have some degree of people-orientation. If it is not possible to recruit these kinds of team members, or if you have no control over who joins the team, one of your first jobs as manager is to make a gut assessment of the "process potential" of each team member. If you find that your team is, by and large, likely to be heavily task-oriented or generally lacking in these process skills, you can then choose between a number of options, such as:

1. You spend the majority of your time building and maintaining relationships among the team members (however, your other stakeholders may not be overjoyed about you spending so much of your time in this way).

2. You recruit an additional team member who is a "process specialist" (assuming that you can find and pay for this person).

3. You spend time and money training and developing these skills in your team members (have you built in enough in the terms of reference to afford you this time/money?).

4. You make do without these skills (in which case, you must be a born optimist or you have very high stress tolerance levels or you don't need to work with these team members ever again!).

Finally, in general, it is thought that the optimal team size (regardless of the nature of its job) is five to seven people. Above seven, sub-teams start to develop and communication becomes more remote or more difficult. If your change project requires a team of more than seven members, you might want to think of establishing, either formally or informally, a "core group", which is relatively small and stable and which branches out to the larger group (see Figure 10.2).

Figure 10.2: A Structure for Large Teams

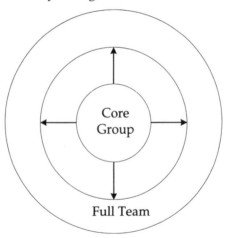

THE LIFE-CYCLE OF TEAMS

Research has shown that groups and teams of all types typically go through the same developmental life-cycle. This life-cycle suggests that, for a team to mature, it must go through a somewhat troubled (but normal) "adolescence". As a manager, you will see your team go through troubled times and smooth times. Knowing the life-cycle of a team will help you to decide whether the trouble in question is a normal part of the team's development or whether it is something more irregular or urgent.

Figure 10.3: The Developmental Life-Cycle of Teams

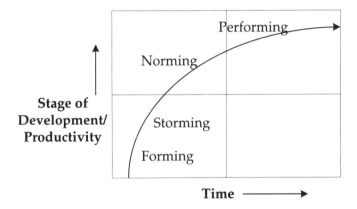

According to Tuckman[1] (who first plotted this typical group life cycle), the following behaviours can be expected in groups and teams at the four different stages:

1. **Forming**: In this stage, the team will be getting to know each other and there will be a fair degree of formality amongst the individuals. There will be a good deal of discussion about "safe" impersonal subjects such as the objectives, the venue, the various rules about who will do what, and so on. Each individual will probably try to make an impression on the others. Soon, however, most groups decide that the formality that was needed at the beginning is too oppressive.

2. **Storming**: At this second stage, personal agendas become more important and the group becomes more "real". There is often stormy discussion about what the group should really be

<hr />

[1] Tuckman, B.W. (1965) "Developmental Sequence in Small Groups", *Psychological Bulletin*.

doing and open disagreement amongst the members. Often, the rules and objectives which were agreed at the Forming stage are re-negotiated. If this disagreement and conflict is handled well, the group can go on to become much more team-like. If the conflict is buried or exacerbated, the group will remain stuck at this stage.

3. **Norming**: All groups and teams need to establish how they will work together. The formal rules which were negotiated and confirmed earlier will fall short of providing guidance on all issues and the team will need to set norms for how they behave towards each other in the informal areas of, for example, how much to disclose about personal fears or hopes, how to take decisions when there is no clear favourite, how hard to work, how to work, etc. Such norms are necessary but usually remain implicit and unspoken. If a new person enters the team at this stage, they will be expected to fall in with the norms and the team may even revert to the storming stage. Norms, however, if unchallenged, have a way of stifling behaviour, especially creativity and novelty. For this reason, sooner or later, most groups/teams will begin to question their appropriateness.

4. **Performing**: Only when the team has made its way through the previous three stages does it enter its mature phase where it is most productive and most flexible. There is very little reliance on rules or norms — they are kept only if they are useful — and things are much more openly and quickly discussed and resolved.

This life-cycle occurs in all groups and teams and, in general, always follows this sequence. However, it is hard to predict the exact timing of when a group will move from one stage to the next as it depends on the nature of the group members, the urgency of the task, the amount of time the group thinks it will spend together, the amount of agreement there is in the group about the task, the size of the group, and the diversity of the individuals who form the group or team. As a team leader, then, there are certain signs to watch out for as they may suggest that the group is stuck in a particular stage:

- Excessive formality — stuck in the forming stage?

- Unresolved tension or conflict — stuck in the storming stage?

- "Groupthink" or unquestioning compliance to "the group's way of doing things" — stuck in the norming stage?

If these signs are evident in your team, the process skills which will be required to un-stick the team relate to communication. You should make the problem (the stuck-ness) explicit and check out with the team whether it perceives any problem. If you are the only one who can see the problem at this point, it might be best to leave things alone for a time as it is not wise to try to *force* a team to progress to a later stage in its life-cycle.

At different points in the team's life-cycle, it is likely that different styles will be more appropriate than others. Of course, as we have said before, the best approach is usually a combination of all styles. In the case of teamwork, a people-orientation includes a recognition of the individual and group dimensions. In general, however, it could be said that certain management styles might be more appropriate at certain stages, as shown in Table 10.1 overleaf (please use this as a rough guideline, not an absolute rule).

INDICATORS OF SUCCESSFUL TEAMWORK

Referring back to Chapter 7 on controlling your change project, it might be useful to think of a number of measures of performance which would tell you whether your team was working well together or not. The measures of performance for teamwork will be predominantly qualitative. Like all measures, they can act as an early warning device. (Sometimes, the easiest way to identify qualitative control measures is to think of the negative side, i.e. what would tell you things were not working.)

Table 10.1: Management Style and Teamwork

Stage in Team Life-Cycle	Predominant Appropriate Management Style	
Formimg	Task-Oriented	Conservative
Storming	People-Oriented	Conservative
Norming	People-Oriented	Developmental
Performing	Task-Oriented	Developmental

There are a number of aspects of good "teamness" which are almost tangible and which can be used as a basis for measuring how well the team is doing as a team. Table 10.2 shows ten areas of team working which can be used as a basis for qualitative control measures, and some simple, but effective, performance indicators (PIs):

Table 10.2: How to Tell if Your Team is Working Well

1. Atmosphere:	The atmosphere in a good team tends to be informal, comfortable and relaxed.
	PI: Team members' own assessment of the atmosphere over time.
2. Discussion:	There is a lot of highly participative talk and discussion but the discussion always re-focuses on the task to be completed.
	PI: Observation of the discussion — is it dominated by one person? Is everybody contributing? Does it get side-tracked or lost up a blind alley easily?
3. Shared View of the Task:	The team will have spent time at the beginning discussing the objectives and reaching a common understanding of what needs to be done and why.
	PI: Regular checking with team members to ensure that they start (and remain) with the same understanding of the team's job.

4. Listening:	The team members listen to each other, regardless of differences in status or regardless of how strange ideas may seem.
	PI: Observation of the team at work. Team member's assessment of whether they think their views are being taken on board.
5. Disagreement:	Good teamwork is not always smooth. An absence of disagreement should not be considered healthy. Disagreement in a good team is handled openly and is resolved by reference to the best solution, not the strongest person.
	PI: Observation of how conflict is handled at meetings — is it buried, swept under the carpet, minimised? Is it resolved according to accepted criteria?
6. Consensus:	There is genuine consensus to decisions rather than mere consent or deference to the most powerful team member.
	PI: Rate of participation of different team members in group discussions. Also, look at when different team members make their contribution — is it always after the most powerful person has spoken?
7. Feedback:	Praise and criticism are informal and frequent and often take place in the public arena. There is no personal animosity when criticism does arise.
	PI: How often feedback is given. Ease of request for feedback. Sensitivity of feedback itself (remember being tough on the problem but gentle on the people?) and of different individuals to feedback about their performance.
8. Openness:	People feel free to express their opinions about the way things are going (how the team is working together and how it is doing in relation to the achievement of its objectives).
	PI: Observation of team interactions. Ask team members how they feel about saying what's on their mind.

9. Action:	The team acts as well as discusses. It is clear to everyone in the team who is responsible for the different actions that are required.
	PI: Does action follow discussion? How soon? How easily? Is everyone clear about the action that is required and who is to take it?
10. Leadership:	The leader of the team (the position may rotate) is not dominant nor is there undue deference to him or her. The leadership of the team is also openly debated and agreed.
	PI: Level, quantity and quality of discussion about appropriate leadership style and role. Type of "followership" that emerges.

Good teamwork does not happen just because a collection of individuals is called "the change team". It will require fairly sustained attention, energy and time, probably yours, for the most part. Don't be surprised if, at times, you find yourself spending a lot of time on managing the team — this is very common in change projects. If possible, schedule in some time into your estimates for this work so that you are not trying to fit it in around your other work. Looking after the team is a real part of getting the job done.

The following tips might be useful in managing your team:

- Try to identify your team members as early as possible so that you can involve them in the objective-setting discussions with stakeholders.

- Always try to have at least one other member of the team with you when you go to meet with stakeholders — bring different team members with you over time. This will allow your team members to develop a wider perspective on what is going on and to understand stakeholder interests.

- Debrief your team regularly and, if possible, in person rather than by memo.

- Allow plenty of time at the first (full) team meeting and, in the agenda for this first team meeting, schedule in personal introductions (ask each team member to speak about their backgrounds and what they hope to get from working on this change project).

- Try not to allow tension to build up — at the end of every team meeting, schedule-in a review ("how are we working together?") or a "moan session" where people can talk to each other about any grievances they might have. Alternatively, if you do not have team meetings, make time yourself to check in with each team member on a regular basis.

- If you think something is going wrong, say so to the individuals concerned. You do not have to know exactly what the problem is, you just have to sense a problem and check it out. It is better to be over-sensitive (i.e. to sense problems which do not exist) than to allow trouble or conflict to fester.

- It is better to err on the side of over-communication (i.e. communicating too much or too often) than under-communication. As we said in the last chapter, communicate about how you feel and about how others feel as well as about the "harder" subjects such as progress towards objectives.

- Finally, enjoy the teamwork — it can be really rewarding (even if it is tough going from time to time) and is usually one of the aspects of working on change projects from which people, including managers, get most satisfaction.

Case Study — The Transportation Task Force

Michael Byrne is a management consultant who specialises in group facilitation. Michael was asked to undertake an assignment with a new task force which had been established to "assist the Minister in drawing up a policy on the transportation of people in the 21st century". The task force was large, with 22 representatives of different interest groups, so a steering group of five people was established to allow for co-ordination and cohesion amongst the task force. The task force is 10 months old and has just produced its mid-term Interim Report. Michael has been asked to facilitate a review meting of the steering group in which the group wants to evaluate its progress and working practices. The following samples are taken from the discussions that took place between the five members of the group and Michael during the course of this meeting.

Michael began by clarifying what the group wanted from this session and by asking them to do a "quick-and-dirty" rating of their progress by giving themselves marks out of ten:

- *"I'd give us a 7. We're doing OK now, we're pretty much on course to finish the job within the time period set for us and I think we'll be able to reach agreement on a set of recommendations for the Minister that really will help to formulate a policy on transportation."*

- *"Yeah, I'd say we're about a 7 too. If you'd asked us this three months ago, it'd have been different but we're getting there."*

- *"I think you're being harsh on us — I'd give us a 9 or even a 10. Given some of the problems we've had, we're doing as well as anyone could expect or as well as any group could do in the circumstances."*

- *"Well, I'm not sure that I'd give us 10 out of 10 but I agree that we'd be somewhere at the top end of the scale."*

- *"Yeah, I agree, I put us at a 7 or an 8 too."*

Michael then took on the role of devil's advocate and asked them why they had not given themselves full marks. He suspected this would lead in to a more general discussion of how the group was working:

- *"Well, it's hard to pin down, it's not an exact science, but I supposed we'd be further along by now, so it's not that we've lost marks by making mistakes, it's just that I expected that we'd have done more or done better by now . . ."*

- *"I feel the same — I feel that we could have achieved more in 10 months than we actually have. In my experience, 10 months to pro- duce a report is a long time. In my company, we'd be lucky to get 10 days to come up with a report."*

- *"Yes, I didn't give us 10 out of 10 because the Interim Report seemed to take us so long to actually get together — it took us a month just to agree on its contents and I think we'd be much further along if we'd just asked one or two people to write it and let the rest of us get on with doing the real work. After all, the Report is just a commentary on work-in-progress, it's not the final document."*

- *"I don't agree, the Interim Report has to flag up all of the issues that we're likely to make recommendations on in the Final Report so it's not just a description of what we're doing."*

He was relatively happy that the group was open to discussing its working practices and internal relations, so he then asked them to list all of the factors that helped the group to work or that hindered the group in its work. He reminded them to bear in mind that they had all rated the group quite highly. The following is the content of the flipchart that Michael ended up with after all five members had listed their factors.

Factors Which Helped	*Factors Which Hindered*
• *Creation of steering group of five — made work more manageable*	• *Very wide terms of reference*
• *Some of the group knew each other and/or had worked with each other before*	• *Some of the group knew each other and/or worked with each other before*
• *Good chairing of meetings and having an external facilitator who was neutral*	• *Competition between different sectors — each sector wanting its own agenda to be prioritised; power plays between members/sectors*
• *Some clarification of objectives early on*	• *Sectoral representatives changed in two cases in ten months*
• *Good secretarial support from the Department — clear and fast minutes of meetings, early circulation of agendas, etc.*	• *Lack of clear feedback lines to sectors so sectors taking a long time to react to proposals*
• *Allowing the disagreements to come to the surface at the meetings instead of elsewhere*	• *Lack of clarity in certain quarters about the role of the group in general and about the role that different people in it were supposed to play*
• *Having the meetings in a neutral venue*	

• *Having sessions like this one where differences can be raised and resolved*	• *Not allowing enough time for meetings at the beginning so having to discuss the same issue at successive meetings*
• *Lack of media interest — allowed us to get on with the job*	• *Lack of media interest — some PR for the group might have drawn more interest earlier on and so prevented some of the lob-bying that went straight to the Minister*
• *Excellent research back-up*	
• *Sufficient resources to allow for field trips to see how other coun-tries are tackling these problems*	
• *Lack of interference by Minister*	• *Creation of steering group — helped get the work done but was divisive*
• *Good balanced sectoral represen-tation within the task force*	
• *Secretary had a "good fix" on all of the individuals within the group and kept up good contact with them between meetings*	• *Nobody was actually assigned the role of co-ordinating the group – it fell between the Chair and the Secretary*

After a good deal of discussion, the group organised these factors into task factors (things which helped or hindered the group in achieving its objectives) and process factors (people, relationships, or working practice-related things which helped or hindered). The following factors emerged as the critical ones for the group:

Task-Related Factors

• *Good knowledge/expertise in group, adequate resources (including time and money), solid relevant research.*

• *Clarification/negotiation of confusing/ambitious terms of reference and of objectives.*

• *Creation of small steering group*

• *No interference from media or from Minister*

Process-Related Factors

• *Good chairing and facilitation of regular review meetings*

- *Some discussion in group about disagreement and contentious issues but not enough open recognition or discussion of power-plays and politics*

- *Need to clarify roles within task force — who is to co-ordinate the group's efforts? What level and type of feedback should there be by sectoral representatives to their sectors/interest groups?*

- *Size of group — 22 people too large, so small steering group created but need to make sure that the other 17 members aren't excluded from discussion/decision-making.*

- *Changes in membership of the group — changes in sectoral representation four months into life of task force caused the group to stall.*

The session was drawing to a close and Michael wanted the group to finish on a pragmatic note so that each participant would feel that they had had a productive and useful day. He asked them to think about how they were going to make use of the work they had done during the review session to improve their task force's work for the remainder of its life:

- *"We have to get our act together regarding the co-ordination — I think we should ask that the Secretary does this — he'd be able to make sure that everyone knows what's going on and that they feel that they're being consulted on all of the issues. I think we should also tell the full group about how we made the decisions about what went in to the Interim Report. I think it's those decisions that are making some of them think that we're doing our own thing."*

- *"Yeah, we have to make sure that we don't end up with a minority report to the Minister — that would just cause endless lobbying afterwards and we'd get no coherent transport policy as a result. But I think that maybe we should do more of the co-ordination ourselves — that way, we'll build better relationships with the others and we'll hear first if there are problems brewing internally."*

- *"I think we should also make sure that there are no more changes in membership — maybe we should contact all of the interest groups, give them feedback about how we're doing, a summary of this session*

even, and ask them not to make any more changes as, from now on,
they could really cause problems."

- *"We also have to address the power-plays and the politics in the*
  group — we can't afford sub-groups and there are definitely behind-
  the-scenes efforts to build coalitions, like the environmentalists ver-
  sus the car users. We have to address these and ask people to bring
  these issues directly to the group where they can be properly debated.
  If one group wins out, the others will never accept the final recom-
  mendations of this task force."

- *"The other thing we have to do is to plan out the rest of our work —*
  we need to do a proper schedule and budget so that we don't run out
  of time and so that we have the resources necessary to make one more
  field trip if we need to. . . . We should also check how much more re-
  search is needed because we might need to look at the budget we have
  for that as well. The earlier we get a properly-costed, detailed plan to
  the Minister, the better. It'll also give him the impression that we
  know what we're doing and that our recommendations are the result
  of thorough research, analysis and discussion."

The group went on to make a number of other suggestions for improving
its working practices. Michael asked them to make sure that none of these
would jeopardise their progress, as there would be little point in getting
better at managing their working relationships within the group, in the
long run, if this caused them to put their achievement of their objective at
risk. The discussion also got a bit bogged down when it came to trying to
reach agreement on who should act on the more difficult steps, like ad-
dressing the power games that they suspected were going on.

However, they had run out of time by this stage and so it was agreed
that the five of them would meet again specifically to look at these con-
tentious issues.

Chapter 11

DELEGATING TO TEAM MEMBERS

INTRODUCTION

Delegation is one of those aspects of management which is almost always considered "a good thing". Yet, in reality, it can be problematic and perceived as being "more trouble than it's worth".

Delegation involves giving a part of the work of the change project to one of the team. Often, we are talking about delegating a part of your (manager) work. In the case of work which can only be done by someone with expert knowledge, delegation is not an option — the work must be done by the expert.

In order for you to delegate part of the project work to one of your team members, the team member must have or be given the necessary *authority* to complete that piece of work (including, where necessary, the authority to secure resources). In addition, it must be clear that *responsibility* for completing the work now lies with this member of the team. However, *accountability* for the results rests with you. Put bluntly, the power to make it happen is given to the team member but, if something goes wrong, the problem reverts to you. This is where delegation can become inherently contradictory: if accountability brings with it a fear of retribution for mistakes made, many of us will hang on to the responsibility and the authority too. A way around the contradiction has to be found for delegation to happen. If it doesn't happen, your workload is likely to become unmanageable.

For delegation to work, therefore, there must be good communication between you and your team member — this communication must be good enough to enable the team member to ask questions, to get answers, and to raise alarm bells in advance of any problem becoming too serious to resolve. It is in your interest to ensure that the team member can communicate all of these because, as we have said, you remain accountable for the results of your team's work.

WHY DELEGATE?

As we said, given that you, as manager, must retain accountability for the work, you might be tempted to opt for doing the work yourself rather than risk delegating it to one of your team. However, for most managers, doing it themselves is simply not an option. Given the time constraints, managers would have to work a 120-hour week to get everything that needs doing done on time. If the change is to be successfully implemented and on time, delegation must take place.

Change project management lends itself very well to delegation because of the "chunking" approach on which it is based. You may remember back to Chapter 4, when we looked at the Work Breakdown Structure of projects, whereby the work is broken into discrete but related chunks (phases → tasks → subtasks → activities, etc.). In addition, we also discussed the need for being clear about the inputs required for each chunk and the deliverables from each chunk.

Much of the delegation that takes place within projects is at the task level (phases are usually too large to be delegated entirely to one person although it is common enough to delegate phases to sub-teams within very large projects).

For example, suppose you are required to write a phase-end progress report for your commissioning clients, and you want to delegate this task to one of your team. The inputs and deliverables of the task that might be included are shown in Figure 11.1.

Figure 11.1: Possible Inputs/Deliverable for a Progress Report

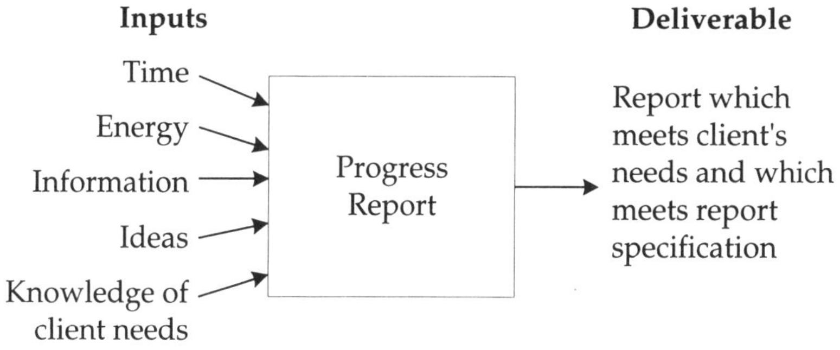

Inputs   **Deliverable**

Time

Energy

Information → Progress Report

Ideas

Knowledge of
client needs

Report which
meets client's
needs and which
meets report
specification

The level of clarity which a good Work Breakdown Structure provides about each task makes delegation easier because there is less room for mis-communication. In the above example, you can make clear that what you are delegating is the production of a progress report to a particular specification, and the resources (inputs) which the team member will need to complete that report are also evident. The only things which have not been clarified yet in this example are (a) the date by which the report should be ready, and (b) what steps your team member should take if they are not happy about any aspect of the task which has just been delegated.

There are three other reasons why it makes sense for managers to delegate some of their work to team members:

1. It saves time for you to do other work, often more strategic work that cannot be done by technical experts or by less experienced team members (e.g. work such as contacts with key stakeholders).

2. It provides a good opportunity for you to invest time in adding value to your staff, as delegation is one of the best approaches to staff development (staff get a chance to "act up" at a slightly higher level than they are used to).

3. It brings more minds to bear on a problem or issue, thereby increasing the number of perspectives and the possibility for creativity.

Your approach to delegation will depend, to a considerable extent, on which of these reasons feels right to you. In particular, your decisions about *what* to delegate are likely to be affected by your view on delegation as an opportunity to save time, to develop staff, or to enhance creativity. This is, of course, an aspect of management style, as we saw in Chapter 8. If your style is to conserve, you will probably feel more reassured by the first of the above three reasons, whereas if your style is to develop, the second and third reasons might be more appealing.

HOW TO DELEGATE WORK

If delegation is such a good idea, why doesn't everyone do it? Apart from some of the obvious barriers (e.g. no one to delegate to), a common reason for managers not to delegate is their fear of loss of control over the quality of work. The issue of control is absolutely central to delegation because delegation cannot happen unless control is also relinquished to some extent.

In every relationship between a manager and a team member, there is a balance between control and trust. This balance is not fixed but the "sum" of the two is. This sum and balance is best grasped through a visual representation, as shown in Figure 11.2.

Figure 11.2: The Trust/Control Balance

Fixed Sum Relationship

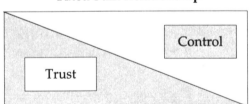

This shows that, for there to be an increase in trust, there must be a decrease in control, and vice versa. It is not possible to increase both trust and control simultaneously. If, by delegating, you are implicitly telling one of your team members that you trust them to do a piece of work, this message will be completely undone if you then apply stricter controls over this person than you apply to other team members.

Therefore, before you delegate, you must establish for yourself how much trust to invest in the other person (and, consequently, how much control to exert). You will probably establish this by reference to the following four variables:

1. Your needs and concerns

2. The needs and concerns of the person to whom you are going to delegate

3. The task itself, and

4. The context.

Table 11.1: Four Factors in Delegation

1. Your Needs and Concerns	• How competent a coach are you?
	• What is your management style?
	• How competent are you at doing the task?
	• How much uncertainty can you live with?
	• How comfortable do you feel about "letting go"?
2. Their Needs and Concerns	• How competent are they now?
	• How long would it take them to learn all the skills required to get it right?
	• How long have they been doing their current job — do they need something new to stretch them?
	• How comfortable will they be doing something new or more difficult than they are used to?
3. The Task	• How critical is the task?
	• How difficult is the task?
	• Who cares about the task (i.e. are key external stakeholders directly involved)?
	• How large is the task?
	• Has it been done before by you or the team?

4. The Context	• How good is your relationship with the person?
	• What is the history of that relationship?
	• What experience do you have of this person's work (quality, speed, style, etc.)?
	• Will you work with this person again?
	• How much time is available for them to develop new skills (if they require them)?
	• Would it create a negative precedent in the team or in your organisation if you were to delegate this task to this person?

Depending on your assessment of these variables, you will have a good idea of how much trust/control is appropriate. In general, unless you know of or have worked with the person before, it is better to start off on the high control side of the relationship because, should you find that high control is not necessary, it is easy to relinquish some control. However, the corollary does not always apply: if you have placed too much trust in the other person and find that you need more control, you may find it quite hard to gain this extra control. Therefore, if you find yourself managing a project where most of the team are new to you, start cautiously and let go as appropriate.

Control can be exercised in two ways in delegation: the first way is dependent on when it is exercised and the second way depends on what is controlled. To make this more concrete, let's refer back to the example of the progress report. How and when would control be exercised or trust be conveyed in this example? The answer depends on where the relationship is located in terms of trust and control. Table 11.2 looks at when to exert control and Table 11.3 examines what to exert control over.

Table 11.2: When to Exert Control

High Control	Equal Trust/Control	High Trust
Before the event — e.g. "tell me when you've got all the information" or "let me see a draft first".	*After the event* — e.g. "tell me when you have done it so that I know it's done and can check up on it, if necessary".	*By exception* — e.g. "get in touch if there is anything unusual about this or anything you need help with".

Table 11.3: What to Exert Control Over

High Control	Equal Trust/Control	High Trust
Control over Inputs, Outputs and Outcome — e.g. "it shouldn't take you more than 10 hours", "use information from this source", "here's what I want the Report to look like", and "I want them to be able to use this Report to justify the amount of funding they're giving us".	*Control over Outputs (Deliverables) and Outcome* — e.g. "here's what it should look like", "it should be no more than 10 pages long, including graphs", "it should show clearly where the money is going and what they're getting for their money".	*Control over Outcome* — e.g. "I'd like you to do a progress Report for the funders — I want them to be able to see where their money is going and how we're spending it."

In this example, we can see that, as the relationship between you and your team member matures (and trust develops), you can leave a lot more to the discretion of the person to whom the task has been delegated. For example, in the high trust situation, you leave everything about what should go into the report and how the report should look to the discretion of the team member. However, it is worth noting that even in a situation of high trust, you do not leave the team member entirely on their own: there is still the safety net of control by exception. The interesting thing about this control by exception, of course, is that it is control which is invoked by the person who is doing the task, not by you. Therefore, it could be said that control has also been delegated.

DELEGATION AND STAFF DEVELOPMENT

We mentioned earlier that delegation is an excellent and commonly-used means of developing staff. It can allow you to add value to your team by building on their existing levels of competence through guided exposure to new tasks and situations.

Just as you would not throw a child who could not swim into the deepest part of a swimming pool, it is not a good idea to ask any staff member to take on a task which is too far beyond their existing level of competence. To develop, there must be stretch and room for growth but, if the gap is too large (between what a person can do now and what they are being asked to do), it will not be bridged. In addition, asking someone to do something where there is a strong likelihood of failure is not going to contribute to the growth of trust between these two people. An old maxim about introducing change is relevant here: "start at the point where you are likely to succeed".

It follows, then, that one of the first things you have to do before you delegate is to check that the person can do the task in question or can acquire the support and resources necessary to learn these skills. In addition, ask the person who you are developing for their view on the level of difficulty of the task — there is no point in you saying "it's easy" unless they say so too. In particular, it is worth noting that one of the drawbacks of the traditional project management approach is that it deals with "resources" (i.e. people) as if they were all the same and interchangeable. However, what is of more concern to a manager who is delegating project tasks is the *resourcefulness* of the individual, rather than the fact that they are listed as a resource.

If you are delegating some task to one of your team, and particularly if this task is partially or completely new to them, it's a good idea to provide them with some sort of backup or support system. The key to an effective support system is that it should be live, flexible and easily available (at least to start with). You need to keep your *brain switched on*, your *eyes open* and your *hands off*. If your brain is on and your eyes are open, you will be aware of what is going on so that, if you are asked for help (i.e. to put your hands on), you can do so easily and quickly. The most common mistakes that managers can make in delegating-to-develop-staff relates to the "support system": the system doesn't work because, for example, the manager does not provide support when asked or the manager provides support when it suits them, rather than when it is needed by the staff member.

In addition, watch out for errors of communication between the two of you (remember Chapter 9?). Using the language of that chapter, you would be the sender and the person to whom you are delegating would be the receiver. Problems between you arise, such as the message that you send is not checked with the receiver, or you don't get any feedback from the receiver about whether the message has been understood, etc. If this is typical of the relationship between you and the receiver, the likelihood is that it will be difficult for the receiver, your team member, to seek your help or support as the relationship so far seems biased towards one-way, top-down communication.

Finally, it is unlikely that you will be met with unbridled enthusiasm from your staff every time you try to delegate something to them. Your staff will resist taking on the new work because they are already working at full stretch to get through their current workload. Or, they may not be at full stretch but they may resist for some other reason. This is where your negotiation skills (Chapter 9) will come in. Between you, you will have to find a way of meeting your objectives (getting the work done) and meeting their objectives (not doing extra work) without doing unnecessary damage to your working relationship.

Extract from Interview —
Manager, Retail Chain

"You were part of the team that brought in a new system of payment in the supermarkets. What was it?"

"The idea behind the EFTPOS system (Electronic Funds Transfer at Point of Sale) was that the public could pay at the checkout with a smart card that would debit their bank account directly."

"Quite a major project, then. How was the system introduced?"

"A cross-functional team was given all the necessary resources, and the authority to run the entire process. The team was headed up by the technical systems manager. His work load was really heavy, and he was going to be held accountable for installing all the processing and IT systems in place, to a very tight deadline. I was seconded from my usual job in the HR department, to carry out tasks connected with internal communications, getting the change message across. Though I was the most junior, and the only non-technical person, I was a full member of the team from the beginning."

"What was it like, working for that manager?"

"He was quite new to the company, so for me, it was an unknown quantity, what it would be like, and at first, I was delighted. We first identified the various parts, the resources and the end-points of each phase. A critical output was the explanatory leaflet. This was to go to each checkout operator and supervisor, and it was important that it was written in plain language and would be widely used."

"Whose responsibility was it?"

"Well, it was an important task from the first phase of the change, something that he was responsible for, but he delegated it to me. I was initially unsure that I could do the job myself. He sat down and we talked through the requirements and my worries. I was afraid that I was asking naive questions and bothering him with trivial matters but when I did bring up any fears or worries I had, he listened. He was really reassuring, and sent me away to think about my task and research how to ensure that the checkout staff would fully understand and successfully apply the new procedures."

"Passing the task on to you must certainly have saved him time, but how could he control the quality of what you did?"

"I got a very clear specification of the length, the style and the layout for the leaflets. He insisted that he would always have time to sort out any unexpected problems that arose. I was able to check back with him regularly about the progress in commissioning designers. He let me know the limits on my budget, and was very responsive to my request to go and investigate some other examples. He actually gave me introductions to other sites where this kind of process had been introduced. Together, we decided to start by piloting the leaflet in a selection of our stores. The two of us met to review progress at regular Friday morning meetings and I remember actually looking forward to the reviews, not as might have been the case earlier, dreading them. For all decisions I had the benefit of his guidance. I also liked the way he took on the accountability. When it was clear that we wouldn't make the initial deadline, because the lead time for the design was underestimated, he didn't blame me, but accepted that we needed to readjust."

"How did you find the experience?"

"I was really chuffed that he was trusting me with such an important early output of the project. By the time that phase of the change was completed, I felt I'd learned a great deal, and was very excited about moving forward, to undertake the actual training programme. "

"Was all your work as satisfying?"

"I'm afraid not. The next job I got was explained only in much more vague terms. He told me he wanted me to prepare a comprehensive training programme to equip the staff with skills to work the new systems. My knowledge of HR issues prompted me to underline the importance of attitude training and preparation for a new role also. The staff to be trained also needed to have an opportunity to rethink their roles, since they now would be responsible for a much wider range of functions in relation to the public. They would have additional responsibilities, and a need to begin to work new procedures, and relate to the customers in a different ways. I had to plan a whole series of steps, and consider many issues, like for instance, how it would affect staff, what training and development needs were arising, the effects on job descriptions and responsibilities, issues for supervision and team work, quality standards, etc."

"What happened?"

"Well, he seems to have thought that because I had done such a good job on producing the leaflets, that it was enough to urge me to be as creative as I was on that occasion. I felt that he had just thrown me in at the deep end. All he did was to re-emphasise what the training programme was supposed to achieve, in terms of outcomes. I think it wasn't so much that he trusted me to get everything right, but rather that his time pressures had grown so critical, and that no-one was attending to a number of decisions that had to be made, especially about the content of the training. In a way, the training programme hadn't been well thought through, there was a hope more than a belief that it would be "all right on the night" because the leaflets had been very favourably received."

"I suppose you fed this back to him?"

"When I met him, he was so pressurised and stressed that he never seemed to have time, and kept saying that he relied on my discretion. He was reminding me that he had to meet the deadline of launching the training programme. He just wanted to be able to sign off that it would happen. We got tenders from a few training companies, and I realised that the request for tenders could get us into real difficulty, since the budgets, resources and other specifications were not detailed clearly enough. We had left too much to the providers, in terms of the numbers they could take through the programme in a given time, we were also settling for the purchase of a very new and expensive training system."

"How did you involve your change manager?"

"It became harder and harder to get his attention. Then, out of the blue, he came one day in a panic to ask me to provide the full outline of the training programme. I reminded him that we needed to specify lots of quality indicators, such as the number of staff completing the course, the cost of training, the staff satisfaction, etc. When I saw his reaction, I realised that we had not been communicating properly. I had to give him feedback, regardless of whether he looked for it, and we had to renegotiate the provision of the training."

Chapter 12

MOTIVATING AND INFLUENCING PEOPLE

The subjects of this chapter are both concerned with how to get people to meet your needs or to do what you want them to do. To begin with, we will look at motivation, which is an important issue for managers in that a demotivated team is less likely to deliver the agreed outcome to the desired specification (time–cost–quality). The second part of the chapter deals with influencing people, which is something that managers do daily, both within their team and beyond it.

MOTIVATION

When we think about what makes a car or any machine work, the answer is usually quite simple: the engine. Yet when we think about what makes people work, the "engine" is much harder to identify. In addition, what drives cars does not vary hugely from car to car but what drives people can have as many variations as there are people.

The study of motivation seeks to explain how behaviour is started and stopped, how it is sustained and how it is directed. Managers often express a concern about how they might motivate their staff better. In an effort to do so, they often try to offer incentives, such as money. Money is usually thought of as one of the main "engines" which drive people to work. Money is important to people yet money is rarely enough to explain fully why people work hard in certain circumstances.

In looking at the motivation to work, three questions have to be asked:

1. What makes people work at all?

2. Once in work, what makes them work harder?

3. In work, what demotivates people?

The answers to these questions are usually different, but are frequently confused. For example, the answer to the first question is, for some people, the need for money but, as we have said, this is not the most common answer to the second question. However, if people perceive that they are not receiving enough money in return for their effort at work, this may account for their demotivation.

This simple example points to a number of variables that must be taken into account in looking at human motivation. Firstly, there must be a *need* that can be satisfied (such as a need for money) and, secondly, both that need and its satisfaction are filtered by *perceptions*. Needs differ between individuals, especially once their basic physiological and security needs have been met, and perceptions are also highly personal and are coloured by factors such as the values learnt at home and at school.

Individual Differences in Motivation

Imagine you have a team of six people plus yourself. There is likely to be some overlap between what motivates all of you and there will also be considerable variation between you. Even if you were all doing the same job, there would be variation because your needs (for recognition, for power, for support, for money, etc.) will be different.

Figure 12.1 lists the "Top 10 Motivators" and "Top 10 Demotivators". These lists are an amalgamation of the work of several researchers into the issue of work motivation and are remarkably similar across a wide range of people and countries.

It is interesting that six of these top motivators relate to internal factors, such as how people see the world and what they value, and only four relate to externally-provided factors (stimulating working environment, money/reward, status and recognition from senior management). These internal factors are called *intrinsic* as they are usually perceived as being an essential property of the work. On the demotivator side, most of the ten items are external (*extrinsic*).

Figure 12.1: Top 10 Motivators and Demotivators

Motivators	Demotivators
1. Interesting work	1. Excessive bureaucracy/control
2. Autonomy	2. Routine/boredom
3. Challenge	3. Not being valued
4. Working in a stimulating environment	4. Terms and conditions of work
5. Money/reward	5. Lack of authority
6. Status	6. Failure
7. Recognition from senior management	7. Lack of feedback
8. Achieving results/success	8. Lack of promotion
9. Responsibility	9. Lack of variety
10. Novelty	10. Lack of job competence

It is worth noting, in relation to intrinsic and extrinsic motivators, that it has been found that extrinsic motivators (such as pay, conditions of work) usually account for why a person chooses to work for a particular organisation but it is the intrinsic motivators (challenge, achievement, etc.) which account for why a person stays there and chooses to work harder. Perceptions and values, as we said, are also important and often account for why a person chooses to work in a particular field or sector, such as engineering or the public service.

The important point here for any manager trying to motivate staff is that, by and large, people *motivate themselves* but are *demotivated by the actions of others*. Therefore, how people are managed does make a difference to their motivation.

Another important point about individual differences in motivation concerns the "grumble factor". This relates to a situation where staff are dissatisfied or morale is low. Typically, what will happen in these circumstances is that staff will grumble about lack of extrinsic motivators (e.g. poor salary, poor terms and conditions of work, over-supervision, etc.). However, it is a common finding of many managers that, in these circumstances, offering more money or improving the conditions in which people work will lead to a short-term increase only in their morale or productivity. This is because people grumble about lack of extrinsic motivators but the real problem is often that something about the way their work is organised is preventing the operation of intrinsic motivators. Therefore, if you find yourself managing a project where morale is low, do not fall into the trap of thinking that simply improving the pay or the terms and conditions of employment of your staff will be enough to resolve the motivational deficit. You may also have to undertake a more fundamental review of why things seem so bad, and this review will probably uncover some deficit in intrinsic motivation (such as boring work, or lack of recognition, feedback or value).

Another way of looking at the subject of motivation is one that is known as *Expectancy Theory*, which states, in summary, that for a person to be motivated, three things must happen:

1.   That person must do something

2.   Some reward must follow that something, and

3.   That reward must meet one of the current needs of that person.

The important aspect of this is that, for the first part to happen (i.e. for somebody to do something), there must be a reasonable expectation by that person that the second and third parts will also hold true (i.e. the act will lead to a reward and the reward is desirable). Thus, all three parts of the expectation must be met: two out of three will not be sufficient to motivate a person.

There is an additional important psychological aspect to this, which is that if a person puts in some effort and no reward follows (or a reward follows but it does not satisfy a need), that person will be twice as unlikely to make the effort the second time around. Put bluntly, the message for managers from this is to deliver on your promises and to make sure that the "prize" is perceived as valuable by the recipient. Remember that the prize does not have to be financial or material — public recognition is often more valuable because people's need for achievement and status is usually quite considerable.

As we have said, much of what motivates a person is not evident to an outside observer (i.e. is intrinsic). This means that the only ways in which you can be sure of knowing what is motivating your staff is to ask them or to observe them very closely over time. In change management, the latter option is not always available. The sum of what mankind has learnt about human motivation is that it is complex, it is diverse and it is impossible to guess or predict in relation to any individual. The advice, therefore, is if in doubt, don't make assumptions, talk to your staff and ask them to tell you what they find motivating and demotivating (and how to avoid demotivators).

Job Design Factors in Motivation

We mentioned above that managers can often make a significant contribution to the motivation of their staff by removing blocks or barriers to the operation of intrinsic motivators.

For the most part, such blocks are not deliberate. They usually arise as an unintended consequence of some aspect of the way work is organised, either at an overall organisation level or at the level of individual jobs. For example, in an organisation with a hierarchical structure, a glut of able people at a particular level might block promotional opportunities for those below them and this block to promotion may become a serious demotivator to some staff.

Jobs that are poorly designed tend to turn off even the most committed people. It is in this area of job design that you can do most to improve the motivation of your team. In general, there are five aspects to the design of any job which you need to consider if your people (and yourself) are going to be motivated:

- Variety — in the work or the skills needed to do the work

- Task completeness — for example, doing a whole task rather than the same sub-tasks or activities again and again

- Task significance — for example, doing a critical task rather than only the non-critical ones

- Autonomy — the degree of freedom and discretion a person has over how the job is done, and

- Feedback — receiving regular progress reports, particularly when things are going well.

As you are probably already thinking, if jobs could be designed with just motivation in mind, it might be relatively easy, but there are, of course, other factors. For example, we spoke in the last chapter about delegation and about the need to manage the trust/control balance — it is difficult to give autonomy or critical tasks over to a staff member that you do not, as yet, fully trust. However, even with new or inexperienced staff, you can look at factors like variety and task completeness.

The subject of feedback is absolutely central to performance management, as we saw in Chapter 7. It is advisable to give staff regular and timely feedback on their performance whether or not your staff are highly motivated. Feedback does not have to be provided in a very formal way — often the best feedback is sincere and honest on-the-spot praise for a job well done. (If the feedback is going to be negative, you may find some help on how to deliver it in Chapter 13). The real power behind looking at how the jobs of your team are designed is so that you can remove any impediments to your staff motivating themselves (intrinsic motivators). It is much easier, and perhaps even more ethical, for managers to allow their staff to motivate themselves rather than for the manager to try to motivate them through the crude application of "carrots and sticks". It also means that you can concentrate on the ends (the project objectives) rather than the means (the motivation of staff to achieve those ends).

INFLUENCING PEOPLE

The use of power and influence is a normal part of the work of managing change or, indeed, of any organisation. Managing change requires a shift, however small, in the balance of power and this shift is usually reached through the influencing of one party by another. This may sound quite Machiavellian. If so, it is not intended to — it is simply stating that, to get things done, managers need to be able to influence people. Influencing people so that they do what you want them to do does not necessarily mean manipulating or coercing them. There are other ways of achieving the same results.

By and large, there are a limited number of ways of influencing somebody to do something they may not want to do. These ways have been categorised into a range of influencing styles, commonly known as "pushing" and "pulling" styles.

Pushing is trying to make the other person do what you want by virtue of your power or rights over them, or your strength of reason. Pulling, on the other hand, involves trying to bring the other person along with you by virtue of your ability to meet them half-way or to attract them to your view. The different types of influencing styles and their associated behaviours are shown in Table 12.1.

Each of these different behaviours can work very well and you can probably easily bring to mind an occasion when you have used them in the past. However, there are times when none of the above approaches seems to work, times when the other person or party seems incapable of being influenced. In times such as these, it is likely that it is not your way of influencing that is at fault, rather, there is something going on in the other person's life or work that is making it impossible for them to be open to being influenced. At such times, trying to influence them might actually just make them more firmly stuck in the status quo. For this reason, there is a third option available: this option involves taking a step back from the other person or party so that they can move back into their "comfort zone". Once there, it will be easier for them to hear what you are saying and, voluntarily, to shift their position on the issue in question. The types of behaviour associated with this option are shown in Table 12.2.

Table 12.1: Influencing Options

Approach to Influencing	Influencing Method	Associated Behaviours
Push	Press (strong push)	• Asserting one's expectations • Applying pressure • Using threats, sanctions and incentives
	Reason (weak push)	• Proposing ideas • Using reason and fact to argue ideas • Evaluating others' ideas
Pull	Connect (weak pull)	• Empathising, involving • Listening and consulting • Sharing feelings and fears
	Engage (strong pull)	• Finding common ground between both parties • Offering a strong vision of a better future

Table 12.2: When Influencing is Counter-Productive

Free Up	Distance (strong)	• Giving the other person "space", stepping back from the situation • Taking "time out"
	Reassure (weak)	• Supporting and helping the other person to feel safe enough to be open to influence

A classic example of when temporarily freeing up is tactically appropriate is when negotiations get bogged down and movement seems impossible as neither side seems willing to concede or "lose face". Very often a half-hour "time-out" at this stage will make all the difference. Similarly, if you are negotiating with a stakeholder or one of your team and seem to be getting nowhere (or even exacerbating the situation), you could consider a temporary withdrawal.

We have introduced the notion here of the tactics of influencing. The real beauty of the categorisation of the different approaches to influencing in Tables 12.1 and 12.2 is that it suggests that everyone has a number of options or "cards" which they can play at different times. However, it must be borne in mind that, typically, each person has a favoured influencing style and they tend to stick to that style quite rigidly. Organisations too often have a favoured style of influencing. So, for example, in large organisations, push styles are often much more prevalent than pull styles (this is often the case in hierarchical or bureaucratic organisations). People tend to be rewarded for using the "house style" so, if pushing is appropriate in your organisation, people working there are likely to learn that pushing is perceived as legitimate (whereas pulling might be perceived as strange).

Regardless of "house styles", it is likely in managing change that a range of approaches will be needed as different situations will require different behaviours. For example, it might be unwise to use a strong push approach (pressing) when trying to attract resources from commissioning clients. In this case, a mixture of the weaker types of pushing behaviours (reasoning, proposing, etc.) and the pull behaviours (involving, consulting, finding common ground) might be more appropriate. Equally, it might be wrong to rely on pulling when trying to deal with a supplier who is late. In this case, the strong push behaviour might be more appropriate.

Often, people find it difficult to vary their influencing tactics. This might be because they lack communication skills (which will limit their potential for pulling) or they feel uncomfortable when asserting their rights. Another difficulty is that managers often believe that they must be consistent, that they cannot push an individual in one breath and then try to pull the same individual in the next breath. However, this is often precisely what is required for effective influencing. Do not limit your potential by always relying on the same approach or believing that, because you started by pulling, you cannot push (or vice versa).

The ability to vary your influencing behaviour is also important because the effect of the different styles on the people you are trying to influence can be very different. For example, the effect of using strong pressure (pushing) is that the person you are seeking to influence may do what you want them to do but only because you have some power over them. In other words, they merely comply with your wishes or demands. On the other extreme, the effect of using strong engagement (pulling) is that you often win the other person over completely, to such an extent that they feel part of the vision and believe themselves to "own" a part of that vision. Using the weaker push behaviour (reasoning) tends to result in a rational agreement or association by the other person, and using a weaker pull (connecting) tends to result in an emotional association. These consequences of the different styles are depicted in Figure 12.2.

Figure 12.2: The Effects of Different Influencing Styles

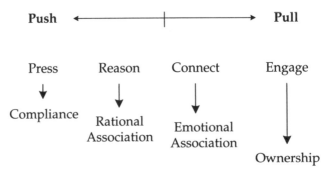

Therefore, in making a choice about which influencing tactic to use at a particular time, take into account the effect that approach is likely to have on the person that you are trying to influence. If you need enthusiasm, commitment and ownership, you need to use a pull style. If, on the other hand, you only need compliance or rational agreement, push styles are fine.

Finally, one last note about the use of power and influence. As we have said, their use is inevitable for change managers. However, how and when they are acquired and used can be important. The following is a list of characteristics of people who are successful users of power and influence:

- They know what others consider to be legitimate in acquiring and using power and influence

- They have a good intuitive understanding of the various types of power and influence

- They develop and use a wide range of influencing styles and they use their influence to gain more influence

- They use power and influence in ways that are tempered by maturity and self-control — i.e. they seldom develop or use power or influence impulsively, and

- They recognise and accept that, in using power and influence, they clearly affect others' lives and they are reasonably comfortable with this.

For many people, it is the last of these five characteristics that can be problematic. Unfortunately, without wishing to sound Machiavellian again, seeking to have other people do what you want them to do is a part of the "job description" for most change managers. If you are not comfortable in achieving this through power and influence, look again at the subject of motivation, in particular, at how to ensure that people work towards your goals because they want to.

Case Study — Change Manager, Technology Company

Peter McCann is Human Resources Manager with a large IT-sector company. Over twelve years, the company grew steadily and had just completed a programme of expansion of their Irish facility. However, the globalisation of the computer industry had meant the arrival of increasing numbers of low-cost entrants to their established market. Management had responded to this increased competition by insisting on a series of changes throughout the company to try to consolidate market share and to streamline its operations.

Peter's own experience of how badly-managed changes had caused huge demotivation amongst staff led him to keep close tabs on how the message was coming across. He wanted the staff to be very clear that their performance to date was mostly fine. However, since the environment had changed, they now needed to show their competence and professionalism by demonstrating how well they could change the way they did business. The best way the change managers could ensure that that happened was to involve all staff in the decisions and their implementation at local level.

Whilst those on the marketing and sales side were fully involved, Peter heard that staff on the production and administrative sides were feeling a bit left out in the cold. About half-way through the eighteen-month change project, Peter launched a scheme to tap into the goodwill and job knowledge that these staff members could offer. The scheme was based on process improvement teams. The team members got training in how to brainstorm good ideas, but not just in a vacuum. Cases were devised to present them with some insights into what was involved in correcting errors and making improvements and about the company-wide implications of some process changes. For example, the administrative staff were asked to deal with a simulated problem involving the investigation of the progress of a supplier's account with errors and omissions, tracking the number of desks it could cross and what the knock-on effect on efficiency would be.

When the improvement teams made a suggestion, they had to support it with analysis, projections and detailed figures. The adjudication of their suggestions was done by the financial and systems experts, not by people's direct bosses. Suggestion schemes had been tried before but this time it was more credible. Senior people with responsibility to make the suggestions work signed off on them which meant that the improvements would be adopted and put in place.

There were also tangible incentives for successful improvements. If a particular suggestion was adopted, the team members that had come up with it would receive valuable rewards for items like stereos and TVs as a token of their successful participation in the scheme. It was equally important to mark their achievement and increase their status with their colleagues. They were encouraged to take an independent and professional approach to anything they observed in their work systems that hampered progress on the change. In the past, excessive control and hierarchy had demotivated people so they appreciated the freedom to make decisions.

As for the section managers, a plan was drawn up to motivate their involvement in the change too and also to extend ownership of the change to them so that they could in turn influence their colleagues. Energetic and committed managers were enlisted into a company strategic leadership group. The group members' new roles and responsibilities entailed having an effective influence on their colleagues at the same level, as well as their junior staff. The group got a briefing that emphasised the need to adapt the way products were being delivered to take account of new stock management systems, and they needed to influence their colleagues to cascade these new approaches down through the company.

They received special training to develop their capacity for strategic thinking and especially for focusing their products to the European market. They also needed to understand the influencing process so as to develop a range of different ways to communicate with colleagues. In order to ensure that everyone was on side, they relied on a number of ways of communicating and influencing: the "normal" ones such as memos, circulation systems and briefing meetings didn't always work and other methods were also required in several cases. Their influencing approaches had to include negotiation, explanation, face-to-face meetings with reluctant colleagues, lots of listening, consulting and attempts to put themselves in the shoes of their staff and constant references to the "big picture" driving the changes.

Finally, they also had to learn how to make acceptable and convincing presentations to outline the logic behind the imminent change and back it up with strong arguments. But they were reminded that, though the change might be driven by rational analysis, there would be emotional reactions to it too. So they learned how to facilitate group discussions and to tune into the concerns and expectations that people were experiencing. They brought people on board by getting everyone to contribute to a vision of the changed organisation, one that built on common values like the good reputation of the company as an employer and, with customers and within the industry, as a producer of high-quality products.

Months down the line, the company had managed to slightly increase market share in Europe and morale had improved significantly. Although staff were happy about the news on the market share, what they were still talking about was the way it had happened and how much they all wanted the company to hold on to this new way of working even when the immediate threat had passed.

Chapter 13

MANAGING CONFLICT AND RESISTANCE TO CHANGE

INTRODUCTION

The inclusion of this chapter is not intended to suggest that all change inevitably involves rows or strife. The reason we have included it is because some measure of interpersonal conflict is a part of working life. Wherever there is a difference between two or more people, there is the potential for conflict. If differences cannot be resolved and conflict is left to fester, it can result in the sort of bad feeling that can make work relations (at least) temporarily miserable.

The focus in this chapter will be on the prevention and resolution of *interpersonal* conflict in changes. To be specific, our focus is not on diagnosing the origins of any particular conflict. Nor is the focus here on finding ways of resolving "hard" conflicts, such as conflicts over resource allocation or scheduling difficulties (the resolution of these types of "hard" conflict has already been examined in earlier chapters (for example, Chapters 5 and 6). The sorts of conflict that we are looking at here are the "soft" conflicts that can occur whenever there is disagreement, diversity or difference between team members (including the team leader). For example, typical of the conflict situations that we are concerned with here are:

- Conflict over breaches of the (formal) rules such as a team member ordering colleagues around, taking too much time off or delaying over coffee breaks, etc.

- Conflict over a team member's work performance

- Conflict over perceived favouritism or victimisation

- Conflict over breaches of the informal rules (often centred around such seemingly trivial issues as leaving the wrong paper in the photocopier).

Typically, in change projects, conflict tends to surface at "pressure-points", i.e. when people are working very hard to complete a phase on time or when a critical task goes wrong or when there is a problem over the budget or when people (resources) are over-allocated. Of course, these are the times when conflict is least welcome as nobody has time to give it the attention it usually requires.

INTERPERSONAL CONFLICT IN CHANGE PROJECTS

Interpersonal conflict can and does arise in change projects, as in any other type of work, for a number of reasons, usually relating to differences that are not resolved. These differences may take the form of personal likes and dislikes or may centre on purely work-related issues.

The following is a brief summary of the kinds of differences that are often cited as causing workplace conflict:

1. **Professional differences**: These are differences in values and/or perspective as a result of professional training. For example, engineers and architects are sometimes accused of valuing design more than value-for-money or even comfort, scientists tend to place a high value on empiricism and rationality and a very low value on emotion and intuition, managers and administrators are often said to be more interested in following the rules or the "bottom line" rather than in harmonious staff relations, etc.

2. **Personal differences**: These are differences in psychological make-up, in style, in opinions, in needs and motivations, in values learned earlier in life, etc.

3. **Priority differences**: These are differences in relation to how resources are rationed — for example, how time is managed, how money is spent, how people are treated, etc.

In reality, conflict is often the result of a compound of two or more of the above types of difference and it can be difficult to disaggregate its cause. All of the above differences are, in fact, differences in values. They may be hard to discuss because, like most things which are over-learnt, many people are not even aware of their "value systems". What is important to remember is that nobody, no project, no organisation is value-free. All of us have values and attitudes, we all bring them to work with us, and from time to time we will find ourselves in opposition to other people's values in the workplace. What we do about this opposition of values is what leads, in some cases, to a healthy confrontation and resolution of the difference or, in other cases, to a long-term, debilitating conflict situation.

APPROACHES TO RESOLVING CONFLICT

Very few people like or take pleasure in conflict. In fact, the balance is usually in the opposite direction, so much so that many people play down their differences in the hope of avoiding conflict.

Conflict may be handled in different ways, depending on its cause. All conflict involves a minimum of two parties or sides. In general, the totality of ways of dealing with conflict can be summarised according to which side starts out and ends up as the winner in the conflict situation.

For example, Figure 13.1 shows the options available to side A if it sets out to win (competition, collaboration, or, at least, compromise). The diagram is useful too in that it shows that there are five possible outcomes to any conflict situation and that all five have implications for both parties' future relationship. The options are not entirely mutually exclusive — tactically, side A may start out trying one approach and modifying this approach as the situation unfolds.

Figure 13.1: Approaches to Conflict

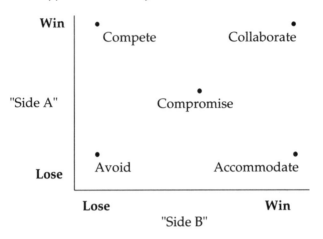

It is clear, therefore, that there are more ways to approach conflict (of any sort) than the simple "I win–you lose" variety. Both parties can lose if the conflict is avoided and both sides can win if the conflict is confronted in a collaborative, problem-solving way. If there is a lack of assertiveness, accommodation is likely to result (one side concedes to the other or accommodates the other's wishes even though they are in conflict with that side's wishes).

Typically, in a conflict situation, we limit ourselves to considering the winning side only. In doing so, we generally limit our options to competing and accommodating (i.e. "I win–you lose" or "You win–I lose"). By considering both sides, we expand the number of options available to us and we can then *choose* which of the five would be most appropriate for a given situation.

The choice about what option to use depends on a number of factors, not just the one mentioned earlier (whether we want to win and how we want the relationship to be afterwards), but also including:

- Who is involved — your approach to conflict with an external stakeholder might differ from your approach to an internal stakeholder

- How much time is available — some of the options, such as compromise and collaboration, require a lot of discussion and consultation which tends to take up a lot of time

- When the conflict occurs — which may have a significant bearing on how much time you have available to you to pay attention to it) and, of course,

- What the conflict is about — how important the issue is to the parties concerned.

Frequently, when people are trying to resolve a conflict, they may overlook the "lose" options (accommodation and avoidance). This may seem very rational — after all, why would anyone set out to lose? — but there are good reasons for doing so in certain circumstances:

- **Avoidance** might be appropriate in circumstances where the conflict is too trivial to risk damaging the relationship (e.g. one of your key members of staff makes a correctable error in a report she's preparing for you) or where, at a particular time, you do not have a chance of gaining anything as a result of addressing it (e.g. one of your staff members is taking a lot of time off because his wife is very ill) or where you feel the particular issue causing the conflict is, in fact, just symptomatic of something else (e.g. one of your staff has started to be regularly late for work but you suspect this might be a sign of a deeper motivational problem and you want to collect more information).

- **Accommodation** might be the right way of dealing with a conflict where you are wrong (e.g. you have been under stress and behaving in an authoritarian manner and your staff are reacting badly) or when it is more important that you maintain harmony than resolve the issue (e.g. you are dependent on someone, for example, to complete a critical phase and you cannot afford to alienate them at this moment) or where the issues are more important to the other side than they are to you — here you can gain "social credits" for conceding on this issue which might be useful later on when there are more pressing issues (e.g. one of your funders is late in making a payment to you but you know this might give you "permission" to be a little late in submitting your next progress report to them).

The key to successfully resolving conflict is to think through to the outcome before you make your move. This may sound obvious but it is amazing how much of our working relationships with others are driven by old agendas, inaccurate assessment of their agenda, and general non-rational behaviour. You need to ask yourself "what would be the effect of me adopting a competitive (or any other) position here?".

Resolving conflict is very like negotiation (see Chapter 9) where you need to consider both the *task* outcome and the *relationship* outcome you want from any particular activity. Just as we said that everyone enters a negotiation situation in order to win, so too could the same be said of conflict. If everybody wants to win, the only way to achieve this ("I win–You win") is to aim for a collaborative approach which generally involves a lot of open communication and the adoption of a proactive, problem-solving stance by both parties. (If neither side can fully win, this is the time to look at compromising).

SOME TIPS FOR MANAGING CONFLICT

Conflict is not an inevitable part of the management of change, but it is a possible one. If anything, because of the explicit and strict targets (for time, cost and quality), change management is slightly more prone to conflict than ordinary management. If conflict does arise in a your change project, what can you do about it? Here are some tried-and-tested tips on how to manage conflict.

Medium/Long-Term Strategies

- Try to encourage an *open, problem-solving culture* in your team, where everybody feels comfortable in being able to say (a) that there is a problem or (b) that *they* have a problem or (c) that you or someone else is causing a problem. Such a culture does not emerge if the identification of a problem leads to a witch-hunt or a blaming session where the "problem is always caused by someone else".

- Agree *explicit standards* for the types of behaviour and levels of performance that are required for the team to work collaboratively (work performance is usually one of the most common causes of change project conflict).

- Have *regular progress reviews* where both the tasks and the relationships are considered — this can often lead to an early identification of any problems that might cause conflict later if left unresolved. In general, the earlier you can identify a potential cause of conflict, the more options you have for managing it.

Shorter-Term Strategies/Tactics

- Develop your *communication* skills, in particular, your understanding of the five key factors in communication (see Chapter 9).

- Consider *all of the options* available to you for dealing with the conflict (i.e., avoidance, accommodation, compromise, competition, collaboration). Make an *informed* choice.

- Gather whatever *supporting information* you can about the issue. However, if the issue is centred on one of your team members, be careful about collecting information from other team members.

- Try to establish *who "owns" the problem* — usually, the problem owner is the person who has or is causing the problem. Many managers intervene to resolve a problem caused by another member of staff. In most of these cases, the best person to resolve such a problem is the person who is causing it. Thus, for example, if one of your team comes to you and says that "it's impossible to work with Thomas, he just does things his own way and it messes up our system", the best person to resolve this conflict is Thomas (the second best person here is the complainant and the third best is you). Thomas's behaviour is, apparently, causing the problem and nobody can change Thomas's behaviour as easily as Thomas.

- Establish what *your role* is to be in dealing with the conflict. If the conflict is between two other people (i.e. you are not directly involved), perhaps you need not be involved at all. In such circumstances, it is more empowering (if slightly riskier) to suggest to the two others that they resolve it themselves or that, if they really need you, your role should just be to mediate or chair their discussions rather than to solve the problem for them.

- When dealing with conflict, be *tough on the problem, not on the people* (see Chapter 9). Confine your attention to the behaviour that is causing the problem rather than attaching global (negative) personality assessments to the person (e.g. if one of your team is bad on the telephone, this is better framed as "Helen is somewhat abrupt with clients when she's on the phone to them" rather than "Helen is just so rude — she has a real attitude problem").

Immediate Tactics

When actually confronting a problem with another person, there are a couple of tactics which can help you (both) to resolve the problem:

- Choose the *time and the place* (for the discussion of the problem) with care and take control by initiating the discussion. There should be privacy and minimal disruption.

- The person (usually the manager) who raises the issue should aim, in the first instance, for *exploration*. It is amazing how often, given enough time, this exploration can lead to (a) either the identification of the problem as a symptom of something else and/or (b) the identification of a solution by the problem owner. A rough rule-of-thumb is that the manager should aim to do about 20 per cent of the talking (consisting of open-ended questions, for the most part), leaving the other person to do 80 per cent of the talking. Let them at least "talk out" their frustration and, with luck, as far as a solution.

- Put yourself in the *other person's place*. When exploring the problem with the other person, try to imagine what it *feels* like to be that person — this will make it easier for you to focus on the problem (and avoid the negative personality assessments).

- Be specific, *ask for change*, and spell out the consequences of no change. The other person needs to know you are serious in requesting a change to their behaviour but you must convey your intention without sounding overtly threatening.

- Be prepared to *change yourself* — you would not be the first manager to discover, on discussion of the problem, that you were partially, or even fully, to blame for causing it. If so, acknowledge it (without being too hard on yourself!).

- Try to end on a *positive note*. Remember, even if the discussion was fractious, you (probably) need to work with the person again so you need to preserve some sense of the relationship.

GIVING NEGATIVE FEEDBACK

One of the most stressful things managers have to do on the job is to give negative feedback to their staff. Telling staff that they are doing a good job is easy; telling them that they need to improve can often be a much more anxiety-ridden task. Yet, as we saw in Chapter 7 (Control), it is not possible to exert an effective control cycle without feedback, and controlling the performance of your most important resources (your people) is paramount.

Here are some pointers about how to handle the giving of feedback:

- Have clear phase-end and task-completion milestones which can be highly motivational as they provide their own feedback on an ongoing basis (and can be used to supplement many of the points below).

- Make sure people know what it is that is being controlled — is it the quantity or the quality of the output, is it behaviour, manner, etc?

- Make sure people know exactly what standard they are supposed to reach — it is surprising how many interpretations people can make of most standards so check for their understanding of the standard by asking them to describe it to you (remember the tips on communication in Chapter 9?).

- If possible, try to ensure that feedback is informal and frequent rather than formal and infrequent. Informality and frequency make it easier to discuss and help to make discussion of performance a normal part of the work of the team.

- Once you have identified to the member of staff the particular aspect of their performance that interests you, ask them to assess themselves in relation to that area of interest before you give the feedback. You will possibly find that most staff members are tougher in their assessment of themselves than you would have been, in which case give them reassurance and help them to improve in that area.

- Focus on the performance, not on the personality.

- Sandwich whatever bad news you have to give in between items of good news or positive feedback about other aspects of their work. This helps them to hear what you have to say (reduces some of the "noise" or anxiety in them) and also helps you see them in a more rounded and balanced way (i.e. you're not just looking at their mistakes).

- Finally, having given them the feedback, allow them time to "digest" it and discuss it. At the end, ask them to summarise what they heard and make sure that they summarise both the good news and the bad news (most people skip straight to the bad news).

DEALING WITH RESISTANCE TO CHANGE

Many managers, all too aware of the resistance that they are likely to meet from their staff and other internal stakeholders in bringing in a change, often feel safer in "attacking" outside forces. For example, it is not unknown for managers to "blame" failed change efforts on their clients ("if only they would change") or on other "outsiders" ("if only they would give me a better budget"), etc. Outside forces are harder to control but usually present less overt resistance — managers do not have to confront them directly and the conflict is general rather than specific. In some cases, managers even identify a "safe" outside force so that they can create a common enemy on which the team can vent its frustrations.

Yet, for changes to occur in organisations, there must be some degree of internal change. There is a commonly-held view that "nobody likes change" and that with change inevitably comes resistance. While these views are probably not universally correct, as a change manager, it is likely that you will have to deal with some resistance in effecting the change. Obviously the resistance you meet will vary depending on the scope of the change, the nature of the change and on how the change is introduced and implemented. The single biggest change that has been brought about in the last 25 years on how each of us works is information technology. The introduction of computers made the work of a lot of people a great deal easier yet was met with a huge amount of resistance in many organisations. People were fearful that they might lose their jobs or be demoted, people were afraid that they would not be able to master the new technology, older staff often feared the advent of the "youth culture" that computers represented, etc. In other words, the introduction of new technology was (and continues to be) one of the most emotional events in any workplace, often leading to a great deal of negative feelings and both covert and overt resistance, even though information technology was almost universally thought of as "a good thing".

If you meet resistance in planning and managing change, it is very likely that this resistance falls into one of the following four causal categories:

1. People resist change because the believe they will lose something of value as a result of the change (e.g. money, status, power, social contact, etc.).

2. People resist change because they have a different opinion about the need for change and/or of the effect of the change.

3. People resist change because they simply do not understand what is happening — a communication breakdown.

4. People resist change because they fear they will not be able to develop the new skills or behaviours that will be required.

As a manager, it is likely that you would deal with these different types of resistance in different ways. There would be little value, for example, in trying to negotiate a salary increase with people in the fourth category as extra money will not affect their emotions.

Six general approaches to dealing with resistance have been identified as shown in Table 13.1.

Table 13.1: Strategies for Dealing with Resistance

Strategy	Definition
1. Education and communication	Teaching, talking with, listening to the person who is resisting
2. Participation and involvement	Working together with the person, listening to their ideas
3. Facilitation and support	Helping the other person to change, giving time and space
4. Negotiation and agreement	Buying the co-operation of the other person, horse-trading
5. Manipulation and co-optation	Persuading (often by offering a mafia-style choice!)
6. Coercion (explicit and implicit)	Forcing the co-operation of the other person

All six of these approaches are effective ways in which to manage resistance. They are not usually intended to be used in isolation of each other: combining two or three approaches usually works best. However, as you can imagine, some approaches work better in certain situations than others and some combine more easily than others. The sorts of criteria that might suggest one approach over another are:

- The amount and type of resistance that is anticipated

- The (authority) position of the change initiators vis-à-vis those who are resisting

- Who has the relevant information and energy for designing and implementing the change, and

- The time available to implement the change.

Each of the six strategies has a cost in terms of time, money and trust. For example, the first three strategies generally take much longer to effect than do the last three and, as a consequence, may end up costing more. However, in return for this higher investment, you generally get a much greater and more durable return in terms of trust and ownership (see Chapters 8 and 12 on management style and influencing style). In addition, as can be seen from the four causes of resistance, dealing with emotion (fear, anxiety, etc.) is usually very important in managing resistance — only the first three strategies make any attempt to deal with emotion.

As a rough guide to the strategies, it is worth noting that if you start at the top (education and communication), it is easy to move to lower strategies if your chosen strategy is not working well or fast enough. However, if you start at the bottom (coercion), it is very difficult to move up to other strategies as you will lack credibility and trust. The lower down the list you start, the greater the risk as your options are more and more restricted.

We have focused very much on the more fraught areas of working with people in this chapter. Again, this is not to suggest that all your change projects are inevitably going to be full of conflict or that you will be giving endless bad news to your staff.

These aspects of working with people will typically only represent a small percentage of your time managing your team. The focus in this chapter on the more unpleasant sides of work should really only be seen as a sort of umbrella — exactly what you need on a rainy day but, thankfully, even in the northern hemisphere, there are more dry days than rainy ones.

Extract from Interview — IT Consultant

"You've quite a track record as a private consultant in IT systems. What's it really like?"

"As you know, everyone says it's a cinch, but in reality it's uphill a lot of the way."

"Have you had a lot of people problems in your change projects?"

"I certainly have. I remember my first one: the local Regional Technical College gave me the contract for the introduction of a Management Information System. The Deputy Director of the college saw it as crowning his career, a key part of the implementation of the college's high-profile strategic plan. He wanted no delay and no hitches in introducing the system."

"So where did you fit in?"

"I was the change manager, and team leader. My personal agenda at the time was to get more business in the education world, so it was vital that I satisfied the client. I started out thinking the job looked quite straightforward."

"Hang on . . . did you select the team?"

"Well, as a matter of fact, it was the Deputy Director who drew up the list. He was convinced that the team needed a strong technical involvement. He proposed Mr Ryan, Director of the Department of Computer Studies, as well as the Heads of Finance, Personnel, Student Services and Building Management."

"What about the user departments?"

"They were represented all right, by lecturers from the Departments of Design, Mechanical Trades and Social Studies. I felt quite certain that we each brought different strengths, and that we could work together as a team.

About two months later, I felt differently, especially after some team meetings from hell. As we continued with the consultative process, gathering data on needs and priorities, we were the butt of bitchy gossip around the college about conflict amongst ourselves, and particularly about my lack of control over the team."

"Was this gossip well-founded? Were you worried that it was a team member leaking it?"

"Both."

"Let's take the first one first, then. What exactly was happening in your team?"

"At that stage, the Deputy Director was getting impatient. According to the schedule, we should have been ready to start the diagnosis, but the data collection was still dragging on. When I started to apply a bit of pressure one day, some team members began predicting that that this project would meet the same fate as other earlier attempts to pool data about the market for RTC services.

Other problems too were beginning to surface — Mr Fagan (Mechanical Trades) wanted to collect his data according to his own specification, and control access to it. Mr O'Neill (Student Services) did not deliver the reports assigned to him. Ms Kelly (Personnel) was worried that staff/performance data would be used to "shaft" people but Ms Healy (Design) disagreed with all this discussion, and wanted to automate the manual records and get on with it."

"Which of them, do you think, was the source of the leak?"

"In fact, we all knew it was Ryan, the Head of Computer Services, who was a crony of the Deputy Director, and who was afraid that his 'empire' would shrink when the others got more IT resources."

"So, how did you feel then? What did you do?"

"I wanted it sorted out. I was pretty worried — I could have ended up in a right mess, and plenty of people would have been happy around the educational system to scapegoat me if it failed."

"Yet up to then you had limited yourself to avoiding the problem and giving in to them. From what you're saying, neither seemed to have been working."

"Yeah, I let it ride for about another week, but you're right, it was getting worse, so I knew I was going to have to do something about it — the problems in the team just weren't going away."

"How did you do it?"

"I took a bit of time to think through what I wanted — I reckoned that there were three main areas of conflict: first of all, people had different ways of working — Fagan, Kelly and Healy had very different work values and interests; then O'Neill's work just wasn't up to scratch and that was having implications for some of the others, and finally, Ryan was breaking the "rules" of the team about confidentiality and keeping things within our own walls. We'd allowed ourselves to drift into a culture of blaming and bickering.

I wanted to take action but, for a while, I didn't know where to start. So I started by meeting O'Neill and told him that he wasn't doing well enough, and I was prepared to help him, provided that he'd started delivering results.

O'Neill was relatively easy. Tackling Ryan was much more risky as I didn't have solid evidence. I also wanted all of the team to be following the same 'rulebook' so I wanted the discussion about Ryan to take place in a team context.

We had an open discussion and it threw up ground rules about how we were to deal with issues like confidentiality, efficient use of time, fairness and an end to the bickering. My job then was to make sure they signed up to those rules. The meeting was pretty tense — there was a lot of straight talking once we got into the problems, yet it helped to bring us together because it cleared the air."

"So, these ground-rules made you into a team?"

"Not on their own but, in hindsight, they certainly helped set us on the right course though it wasn't quite all plain sailing from then on."

Chapter 14

THE CHANGE MANAGER AS CONSULTANT

INTRODUCTION

Managing change and consultancy often go together. In fact there is a whole industry revolving around change management consultancy and you may already have experience of working with consultants on other change projects within your organisation. Typically, we think of consultants as being external to the change team, people who are brought in from another part of the organisation or from specialist consultancy firms to provide assistance.

There is another dimension to change management consultancy, one that is becoming ever more prevalent, and this is where the change manager is seen as a consultant on their own change project. The reason this view of change managers is gaining ground is because managing change can benefit greatly from a consultancy approach and because experienced change managers are often called on to lend their expertise to others who are managing change (sometimes a large fee is even attached!).

So far, we have not defined what we mean by a consultant. This is because the term "consultant" has come to mean many things, from the expert advisor to the process facilitator. In the next section, we will look at the different types of consultancy roles that any consultant may play but, for the moment, when we talk about consultancy we are referring to *a process of communication* whereby the consultant sets out to explore what their clients have in mind and then goes on to help to deliver the outcome which the clients want.

It is important to bear in mind that it is not the consultant who has the direct power to make changes: it is the person who "invites the consultant in", usually the client. Thus, for consultancy to work, there must be some degree of collaboration between the client (who has the power to change things) and the consultant (who has the power to help the client to implement these changes).

For example, suppose you work in a retail organisation and your senior manager commissions you to introduce a change in opening hours so that you can become more competitive. As a consultant/change manager, your chances of introducing the right change in the right way will increase dramatically if you consult with your stakeholders, such as with your senior manager (to find out what impact the change is supposed to have — increased market share? higher turnover? greater efficiency?), with clients (to see what changes they would like — perhaps they would prefer better quality or a wider range of goods more than longer opening hours), with staff and their unions (what concerns might they have in relation to this change?) and so on. Figure 14.1 provides a generic depiction of you in relation to your stakeholders in managing such a change.

Many of the potential benefits inherent in the consultancy role are secured through *communication skills* (see Chapter 9) and, in particular, by making sure to ask the right questions (i.e. questions about objectives and outcomes (see Chapter 2)) of the right people. In addition, the best consultants *assist rather than direct* (unless they are explicitly called upon by their clients to be directors). Of course, the consultant cannot consult unless they have *access* to the right people.

The benefits of playing this consulting role generally outweigh the risks or costs associated with it. We have spoken several times before about the importance of managing relationships in change. Consulting is one of the most effective ways of building trust and good working relationships between you and the different stakeholders involved in your change project. In complex changes, where there are multiple clients and stakeholders, it is only by consulting with clients and stakeholders that you can gain a clear idea of their objectives and a clear perspective on the problem you are being asked to address. If the objectives of different clients and stakeholders are different, again, it is by consulting with them about these divergences that you can help them resolve their differences. In a sense, consultancy is the best route to ensuring that the change addresses the right issue in the most appropriate way.

Figure 14.1: The Job of the Consultant

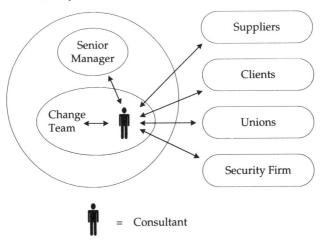

CONSULTANCY ROLES

As a consultant, you can adopt a range of different roles. It is usually most helpful if the consultancy role is chosen by reference to the particular client or stakeholder who is being consulted at that moment. The most important indicator of which role is most appropriate is the type of assistance that the stakeholder wants at a given time. For example, some will want the consultant (you) to "just fix the problem", others will want the consultant to help them define the problem, others will want the consultant to provide ideas as to how the problem might be solved. As clients often do not make these wishes explicit, however, you have to keep an open mind for much of the time.

The different consultancy roles that you can adopt can be seen in Figure 14.2. In essence, there are three styles, ranging from client-led through to client-consultant partnership and on to consultant-led. (Here, the word "client" refers to anyone who requests the help of the consultant in addition to end clients and commissioning clients.)

Figure 14.2: Consultancy Roles

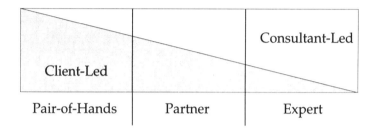

| Pair-of-Hands | Partner | Expert |

- **Pair of Hands**: In this case, the consultant (change manager) is brought in to be an extra resource to the client. However, this resource is treated by the client as just another pair-of-hands. The *client retains full control of decisions and initiatives* and the consultant responds to the client's diagnosis and proposals. The consultant's goal is to make the change more efficient by the application of their knowledge or experience. The client remains relatively *independent* of the consultant.

- **Partner**: Here, the client and the consultant (project manager) *collaborate in a joint undertaking* involving the diagnosis, selection of a solution and implementation of the chosen solution. In this role, the consultant does not solve the problems for the client, but applies their special skills to help the client solve the problem so that it stays solved. There is *interdependency* between the client and the consultant.

- **Expert**: Finally, in this case the consultant is brought in by the client in order to diagnose and solve the problem. In this kind of relationship, the *client often elects to play an inactive role* and the consultant accepts responsibility for solving the problem.

Collaboration is not required as the client has, in effect, delegated the entire matter to the consultant. As a result, the *client is dependent* on the consultant to fix the problem.

The choice of which of these roles to play in any given situation depends on criteria such as:

- The client's need or wish — if unexpressed, part of your job as consultant is to explore it

- Your preferred style — not to be underestimated as this is where you will unconsciously start

- The nature of the problem — what sort of knowledge, expertise, experience, attributes, etc. are required to solve it and which of these does the client possess?

A fourth criterion is important too, particularly in any field which espouses the principle of personal development, and that is the degree to which *transfer of learning* is required (from consultant to client). As you can imagine, there is very little transfer of learning in the Expert role which means that, if the problem (or any variant of it) recurs, the client is once again dependent on someone to fix it for them. Equally, there is very little transfer of learning in the pair-of-hands role as very little is required.

It is the collaboration entailed in the partner role which is most beneficial to the client if transfer of learning is required because the client learns the skills involved in consultancy as well as the skills involved in diagnosing and remedying the problem. However, on the negative side, the Partner role is often the one which is most time-consuming and is not appropriate in a crisis.

STRUCTURING THE CONSULTANCY

Regardless of which of the above three consultancy roles is adopted, there is a fairly generic sequence of stages which consultants follow in their relationship with their client. The five stages, and the activities which the consultant needs to engage in during each stage, are detailed in Table 14.1 overleaf.

Table 14.1: Stages in Consulting and Associated Activities

1. **Entry**	• Exploring the problem and different stakeholder's perceptions of the problem.
	• Clarifying client/stakeholder expectations of you (and your team) and clarifying and negotiating your role.
	• Outlining the Terms of Reference.
2. **Exploration/ Diagnosis**	• Deciding what information is needed (quantitative and qualitative) and negotiating access to it.
	• Dealing with any issues about the collection of data (such as how to collect the data and the availability of the required collection resources).
	• Analysing the data according to some agreed criteria/performance measures.
3. **Agreeing a Solution**	• Giving feedback to the clients on the diagnosis of the problem.
	• Dealing with any resistance from clients or other stakeholders.
	• Planning a course of action.
	• Putting control systems in place.
	• Supporting, motivating and influencing stakeholders.
4. **Implementation**	• Re-negotiation of your role as consultant (e.g. how much involvement is expected of you during the implementation? Can it be delegated?)
	• Troubleshooting the solution with the client with reference back to stakeholders' objectives.
	• Communication, communication, communication. . .
	• Transfer of learning to client (if appropriate).

5. Closure	• Signing off (make sure it happens!)
	• Agreeing access by client to you to ensure client's security in case of unforeseen problems with the solution which has been implemented.
	• Evaluation (of both the consultancy process and the effectiveness of the solution).

CONSULTANCY SKILLS

Nearly all of the skills required for effective consultancy have been discussed in earlier chapters of this book. In particular, the skills associated with communication and negotiation are vital to good consultancy. Table 14.2 represents a summary of some of the behaviours to be effected and some to be avoided in being a consultant. In looking at these skills, rate yourself (mark yourself from 1-10) on each in terms of your comfort in behaving in these ways. This will give you some insight into your own strengths and weaknesses as a consultant.

In addition to communication and negotiation, delegation, planning and control, identifying and managing stakeholders, and motivating and influencing are the main competencies you will need to be an effective consultant. Other skills mentioned in the table are often latent and emerge or evolve quite naturally through experience and exposure (e.g. ability to talk about money and to deal with clients in positions of high authority, etc.). The remaining skills (such as the ability to be patient, to avoid competing with the client or creating a dependency, to support and counsel clients when they need it, etc.) will come with experience of the consultancy process itself. These "pure consultancy" skills are widely applicable to other areas of management and so are well worth developing in any case.

Table 14.2: Summary of Consultancy Skills

Behaviours and Activities	Your Rating (from 1-10)
Predominantly Task-Oriented	
❑ Ability to manage time.	
❑ Skill in collecting and analysing information.	
❑ Willingness to help clients to identify their own problems and desired outcomes.	
❑ Ability to probe client so that client identifies outcome that is wanted.	
❑ Skill in feeding back to client data collected about the client's way of working in such a way as to facilitate client to change.	
❑ Ability to get ideas across to another person clearly and effectively	
❑ Willingness to negotiate with client over access to sources of information	
❑ Ability to help client formulate policy and work out in advance the possible consequences of his or her decisions.	
❑ Skill in monitoring implementation of plans and adapting them to unexpected emergencies or changes.	
❑ Ability to talk about money without embarrassment.	
❑ Ability to set realistic goals and to encourage client to do so too.	
❑ Ability to confront difficult issues.	
❑ Ability to relinquish ownership of the project.	
Predominantly People-Oriented	
❑ Listening and clarifying what other person is saying; asking open-ended questions.	
❑ Willingness and ability to see things from other person's point of view.	

- ❏ Ability to pick up and follow up on the underlying feelings in what another person is saying.
- ❏ Ability to handle disagreement with client.
- ❏ Ability to support and build confidence and security of client so that they can do more.
- ❏ Ability to build trust and credibility.
- ❏ Ability to vary influencing behaviour to suit client needs.
- ❏ Ability to delegate.
- ❏ Ability to judge the culture and climate of a meeting.
- ❏ Comfort and effectiveness with clients in positions of high authority.
- ❏ Ability to transfer skills to client.
- ❏ Ability to discuss openly the workings of the client-consultant relationship with the client.
- ❏ Ability to avoid giving unrequested advice.
- ❏ Ability to avoid "always being the expert".
- ❏ Ability to find out why client is resisting (an idea or a proposal) rather than seeking to persuade client or arguing with them.
- ❏ Ability to let client see their limitations (i.e. to avoid over-praising client).

MANAGING EXTERNAL CONSULTANTS

We are now going to turn to looking at the other side of the consultancy experience, that is, to using external consultants on your change project. You might, for example, bring in outside specialists to assist you with local publicity or with some highly technical aspect of implementing the change you are managing. In fact, even using outside professionals such as accountants and lawyers can be considered as employing consultants and the ideas which follow apply here too.

One of the principle reasons that managers use outside consultants is because it is often perceived to be cheaper, easier and quicker to source some types of expertise from the outside than it is to get it from within the organisation or to develop it locally. This is certainly the case for experts or specialists such as lawyers or accountants. Most change teams will not have a fully-trained lawyer or accountant in their midst and it would take years to develop such expertise.

In other cases, there are political trends (world-wide) towards "downsizing" organisations which have brought the employment of "consultants" (i.e. staff on short-term contracts) into the realms of normal practice in some sectors and industries. Whatever the cause, what is not in dispute is that managers rely more and more on the employment of consultants to get their change projects completed to specification. This means that managing external consultants can be another key activity for change managers.

The advice shown in Table 14.3 represents a distillation of articles in management journals, involving a range of managers from both the private and public sectors, about how to get best value from external consultants.

Table 14.3: Getting Maximum Value from External Consultants

Be Sure to . . .	Try to Avoid . . .
• Be clear about what you want them to do. • Shop around and set selection criteria in advance (do you always want the cheapest or the ones with the biggest reputation?). • Talk with them at the earliest possible stage about what their full range of charges is. • Invite the consultants to visit you in your place of work so that they get a "feel for things".	• Over-selling the job that you want the consultants to do — if you just need a bicycle, don't suggest a car (you will end up paying for it!) • Having the consultants work in your offices — this could turn out to be an overhead cost that you could well do without. • Specifying a price but not a time or level of quality — use the time-cost-quality triad to agree the terms of reference.

• Have a written contract with them and include penalty clauses and liability.	• Competing with the consultant — if they are the experts, let them be the most expert.
• Agree performance measures and milestones with the consultant.	• Lying to the consultant.
• Check that the consultant has the same understanding of the job that you do.	• Unnecessarily involving the consultants in the internal politics of the organisation — remember, politics will tend to confuse things for the consultants, therefore it will take them longer to do their work and you will pay more for their services.
• Try to get references (of previous clients) from the consultant and check them. Visit the sites of their previous consultancy assignments and talk to local managers.	
• Monitor the consultant's progress and agree a regular reporting structure.	• Paying for the senior partner or most expert of the consultants and actually receiving the services of the apprentice or juniors in the firm.
• Insist that the consultant speaks your language, not jargon.	• Try to ensure that the consultant is not just imposing a standard solution if what you need is a customised one — there are many stories of getting the same "Triple A Consulting" solution regardless of what the problem is.
• Keep a log of your experience of the process: it will help you learn and could be useful if anything should go wrong.	
• Following completion of the consultancy assignment, debrief your staff or other stakeholders about the experience.	

THE PROCESS OF CONSULTANCY

Much of this chapter is a consolidation of concepts, points and approaches that have been introduced in earlier chapters. The change manager is, of necessity, a many-headed creature, all of which can be subsumed into the role of consultancy.

Consultancy is a process, not an exact science. Like most processes that relate to managing people, it is usually better that the process is begun and maintained, even if mistakes or problems occur within it, than not begun at all. You already have a wealth of communication skills and judgement in managing change. The detailing of the process of consultancy in this chapter is intended, therefore, to be treated as a supporting checklist for your change management process, rather than as a new set of skills to be acquired. The best advice is to keep your eyes, ears and mind open throughout this process and to use your judgement if unprecedented circumstances arise. Your learning, experience, expertise and judgement have taken you this far in your career. The consultancy approach will sit well on this foundation as it is designed to sharpen your antennae and to encourage you to seek a more exploratory and proactive role in your management of change projects.

Extract from Interview with Change Consultant — On the Nature of His Culture Change Assignments

"Tell me about the most satisfying aspect of your work as a consultant."

"The change was driven by senior managers, but what really made it stick, and catch on, was the way it was branded internally. All the different steps fitted together in an identifiable whole. Everything that happened was clearly visible and seen to be part of the change programme, so even if one step happened quite a long time after the other, it wasn't greeted with cynical comments like "I thought that had run out of steam, it's been so long since we heard anything."

"What was your actual job in driving this change?"

"The major element that we took responsibility for was the development of a different mind-set amongst the managers, and as a consequence, a different way of behaving. It went quite deep, into people's perception of themselves, and their career prospects, so it needed sensitive handling. We used internal research to identify four core values that were needed if the company was to stay competitive. They were exemplified by thirty-odd managerial practices. The staff that reported to them measured managers' performance on these practices and the results were processed by an independent organisation, and fed back in confidential sessions to the managers, so in fact it was a huge feedback loop."

"Who had access to this sensitive information?"

"One of the biggest difficulties was how to gather data that had high credibility, and yet wouldn't be used, or perceived to be used, in a threatening way. If people were too uncomfortable or scared, they would not have co-operated, and then the change would have taken much longer to bring in. Also we would have needed to provide massive resources to compensate staff for the changes to their working conditions."

"Quite scary, for the individual managers, all the same . . ."

"First of all, we secured a high level of trust by holding the data outside the organisation under independent control. The profiles were fed back to individual managers, as part of a development event that also gave a context and offered support for their learning. They attended a week-long programme to develop their understanding of the key practices, and increase their ability to use them in their everyday work. They ended up with specific individualised action plans, to implement these practices."

"You often get a high level of enthusiasm just after those events, but it runs down later. Did this happen in your change?"

"I mentioned feedback loops: we anticipated the necessity of closing the loop. Arrangements were built in, giving the managers the opportunity, a few months down the road, of re-running the questionnaire and reviewing their progress on the action-plans they had committed themselves to at the first workshop."

"What would have been the most significant insights that managers took away from this process?"

"Well, it was amazing that they often got it wrong about their own practice. For example, they gave themselves credit for practices that their staff never saw, and on the other hand, they ruled out some others that staff actually identified in them."

"What sort of success was achieved? What were the outcomes?"

"Well, we were very satisfied because over 90 per of them came back for the follow-up workshop."

"For you personally, at what point did you recognise that the change would take root, despite the cynicism expressed about earlier efforts?"

"I think it was when people started making the change their own, and began suggesting practical ways of innovating with the service. "

"You've been talking about what the managers learned. What about yourself?"

"I think it underlined for me the importance of having the unshakeable support of the CEO: without that, we could have called the whole venture off. Secondly, the role we had as internal consultants was to be partners with branch staff and central functions. Thirdly, no-one could opt out or remain unaffected: they could take initiatives in a flexible way, provided they shared a firm understanding of the vision for change."

Chapter 15

MANAGING CHANGE:
LAST THOUGHTS

INTRODUCTION

The reason we are finishing this book with another look at managing change is to return to a "big picture" perspective after the detail of the various aspects of managing change and to consolidate your change management practice with some tips passed on from other change managers who have come through the process and "lived to tell the tale".

This book is an attempt to structure complex or unprecedented change so that it is easier to manage and control. This structuring usually consists of trying to break down the complexity into manageable chunks: control is exerted over the chunks so that the overall change is kept on course. Successful change management is most likely when there is a balance of attention to the "small picture" (the chunks) and the "big picture" (the strategic objective of the change).

Many of the ideas you will meet in this chapter will not be completely new to you as they were introduced earlier. We will be looking again at some of the concepts encountered in Chapters 1–2 and 12–13 (problem definition and scoping, project control, communication, negotiation and delegation) but, in this case, we will look at these concepts from a slightly different (bigger picture) angle.

MANAGING UNCERTAINTY

We spoke in Chapter 3 about the uncertainty inherent in most projects or attempts to manage change. As we have said earlier, this approach to managing change seeks to make certain as much as possible in advance of the implementation of that change (e.g. the scope of the change, the desired outcome, resources available, etc.). This incorporation of many of the techniques of "old" project management offers an attractive approach for many managers. Yet this very strength can be a weakness in that the attention to planning, structuring and controlling can give the illusion of much greater predictability than is really the case.

Given that there is always an element of uncertainty in managing any change, one way of trying to deal with this is to separate uncertainty about the *direction* ("where are we trying to get to?") from uncertainty about the *process* ("how will we get there?"). As you can imagine, the most difficult change projects are those where a change is required but there is double uncertainty. A simple matrix can often provide guidance as to how to manage change while taking account of uncertainty, as shown in Figure 15.1.

Figure 15.1: The Uncertainty Matrix

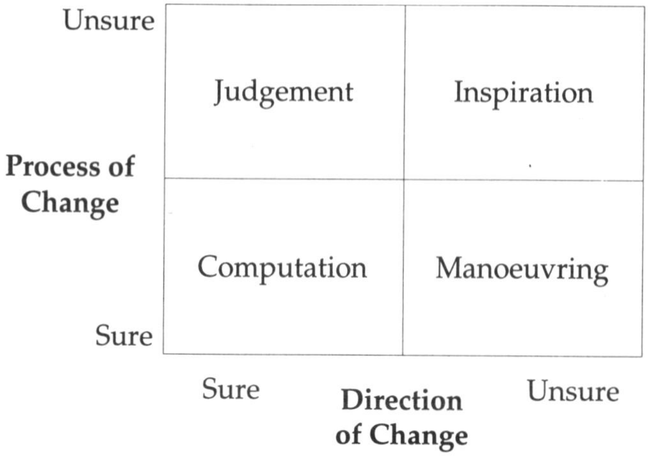

	Sure	Unsure
Unsure	Judgement	Inspiration
Sure	Computation	Manoeuvring

Process of Change (vertical axis: Unsure to Sure) — Direction of Change (horizontal axis: Sure to Unsure)

If, as a change manager, you (and your stakeholders) are sure of what you are trying to achieve (the direction of the change) and sure about how to get there (the process), you are in the fortunate position of being able to "compute" the change. On the other hand, if your stakeholders cannot give you a clear idea of what it is they want and they are not sure about how to get there, you are in the realms of management-by-inspiration, and it is important that your stakeholders are aware of this. Often, stakeholders want to buy "computation" but only provide (or are asked for) enough guidance to afford judgement or inspiration.

Obviously, if the entire change is in the area of inspiration, it is going to be difficult to manage. Stakeholders, especially senior management, often attempt to move everything into the computation or (as a second choice) manoeuvring areas. Unfortunately, some change management scenarios will be difficult to fit into these various boxes. It is a mistake to try to compute what must be manoeuvred, or to try to manoeuvre what must be judged, or to judge what can only be inspired. Make sure that you check and review which box you are working in, and what might cause you to move out of it. It is unlikely that you will find yourself looking at inspiration as the only option available to you: in most cases, at least parts of the projected change can be approached through computation, manoeuvring and/or judgement with some degree of certainty. For example, suppose you have been asked to manage a change project concerning the introduction of company-wide staff performance appraisal. You are not sure what it is that your Managing Director is trying to get out of this scheme (is it a new way of exerting control over the staff, or perhaps of getting higher performance from them, or perhaps it is intended to be a problem-solving tool or a staff development measure?). What is clear is that you are not sure, in this case, of where you are trying to go. This implies that computation and judgement are not really available to you unless you can find out more about where it is your MD wants to get to. Given the level of suspicion or just puzzlement that may surround the change once it becomes public amongst the staff, you may have to do a lot of manoeuvring of staff representatives, unions, key people, etc. just to get them to comply (let alone agree with) the proposal.

The key is to take some time to analyse the nature of uncertainty when you meet it, and then to proceed as appropriate. Don't be afraid to use your judgement or to admit to waiting for inspiration if this is the only option available — part of being an effective manager is to manage other people's expectations and it is usually better to under-promise and over-deliver than vice versa. You need to keep in step with your stakeholders. Yet often, in reality, you may have little choice than to act in the face of high uncertainty because stakeholders are relying on or pressurising you, or because they perceive no option but to embark on the change regardless of the uncertainty.

The good news, though, is that action will give more information and so increase your chances of successfully dealing with the uncertainty. Action does not mean rushing blindly in but, rather, taking time to understand the context of the change, integrating hard and soft information, and then acting accordingly, whilst being aware that uncertainty will continue to crop up right throughout the change.

MAPPING OUT THE CHANGE

Achieving a grip on a highly uncertain change scenario demands the sort of rounded understanding that we have been arguing is the essential complement to your technical skills. It means looking at the situation as a whole, and at the same time from many angles, trying to see both the wood and the trees, cutting to the core of the matter. The more complex the change, the more difficult (and more vital) it becomes for you to gain this rounded understanding.

Many of the change projects that managers are asked to undertake do not lend themselves to clear-cut solutions. To use some jargon, these changes are messy and have no clear boundaries. This means that they show some (or even all!) of the following features:

- A large number of stakeholders with diverse interests

- No single cause-and-effect relationship of the environment and the problems

- Irrevocable practical steps have to be taken under conditions of internal conflict and external pressure

- It can be difficult to find an entry point because several problems are interacting together

- The change is presented as unavoidable because of conditions in the environment

- Many factors are unknown, intangible or unpredictable

- The high risk of failure can make it a leap into the unknown

- The problem does not have obvious beginning and end points and is difficult to remove from its context

- You may have difficulties establishing your own credentials and power-base

- People perceive that the change will bring them costs, not benefits.

It is clear that messy, unbounded changes do not lend themselves to being tackled in a simplistic way. For changes resulting from, for example, greater scrutiny by government or tighter regulations at EU level or declining market share or increasing competition or mergers of companies/organisations, we would need to identify as many as possible of the contributory factors and stakeholder interests. This is known as "mapping" the change and, very often, it is best done by using diagrams rather than verbal descriptions or lists only.

Diagramming is not necessarily a highly technical skill: everyone can draw diagrams. The purpose of diagrams is to identify or map out as many as possible of the different aspects of the problem requiring the change. It does not have to be neat or even self-explanatory — it just has to serve as a prompt to you to the various possible causes and/or consequences of a particular issue.

There are many forms of diagrams but, in our experience of mapping change, often the simpler diagrams are the best. We have used some of these types of diagrams in this book so you will be familiar with them already (see, for example, Figures 3.1 and 7.1 for simple diagrams of the different facets of setting objectives and control, or Figures 4.4 or 11.1 for examples of simple input-output diagrams). The main purpose of diagramming is to help ensure that the problem or issue is mapped out in its entirety so that a solution or solutions can be chosen and prioritised. Your diagram is not intended to *be* the solution, but to help ensure that you choose the right solution on the basis of a fuller understanding of the problem.

Case Study

The management team of Purair was meeting to discuss the recent decline in its profits. They thought there was one main causal factor: that they did not understand their competitive environment. This was an issue over which the company had some control so the management team decided to examine it in greater detail. It was the new marketing director, appointed with a brief to turn the company around, who suggested to the team that they all get involved in mapping out the problem. The exercise concentrated their minds on the scale and gravity of the problem facing them. The marketing director got agreement that where they needed to get to, at least in the short term, was a halt in the market decline. Deciding how to get there was more contentious. His judgement — that they prioritise the sales force–customer relationship — was initially rejected by his colleagues. However, talking through his judgement on the problem and the priorities for solution through the mapping exercise increased the chances of his success and ensured that, eventually, they were all committed. The map that they drew is shown as Figure 15.2.

Figure 15.2: A Multiple Cause Diagram for Purair

THE RATIONALITY AND POLITICS OF CHANGE

Even if you have mapped out a complex change, it is easy to fail to give enough attention to the softer data. Remember Chapter 13 on resistance? When a well-intentioned, and perhaps urgently needed, change project has gone wrong, people often say that it was thwarted by politics or by the organisation's culture, with the inference that the change manager can do little about these. We would argue against such defeatism and, at the same time, alert you to the importance of taking into account the cultural, political and emotional "lie of the land" before and during the change you are managing. This so-called soft data is an important part of what you need to know (it is not just something that would be nice to know). The messier the change, the more essential it is for you to integrate the soft data with the systematic and rational techniques which we presented in the first half of this book. They will serve you well in helping to ensure that you don't omit anything of importance, and can also be useful when justifying actions and decisions at a later stage. However, you will also need to apply these techniques flexibly, within the context of political realities.

You will find it useful to think through who is going to be affected by the change and how they are likely to perceive it. This is not as complicated as it sounds. A good deal of research into change suggests that there are five essential requirements for success in managing messy change — Vision, Incentives, Competence, Resources, and Action (VICRA). So use the VICRA checklist to focus your use of the techniques and leadership skills which have been presented in earlier chapters.

Vision

We have already mentioned the importance of bringing in the support of senior managers for change projects. They can make a huge contribution by developing and communicating a vision about the change. People on the receiving end of the change will be more receptive if they are clear about the rationale and they are more likely to contribute in a positive way if the vision harnesses the change project to needs and values that they see as important.

Incentives

If work practices are going to change, people want to know what benefits the change will bring to them. Incentives that are meaningful for the people concerned (pay, of course, but also working conditions, career opportunities, work challenges and stimulating work, remedies for current difficulties which they are encountering in the work, etc.) help to prevent them from resorting to delaying tactics.

Competence

When change is mooted, people at the receiving end often have concerns that the type and level of skills and knowledge that they have relied on up to now will no longer be relevant or sufficient. It is frequently true that new skills need to be acquired, sometimes at short notice. Systematic development programmes can upgrade skills, knowledge and even attitudes, whilst reducing anxiety by linking in some areas of continuity.

Resources

If they are to put their new competence into action, people need appropriate equipment, budgets, information and staff to enable them to deliver on the aims of the change project. If these resources are not made available, those on the receiving end will be frustrated and may sabotage the project.

Action

A realistic plan needs to be put in place and implemented at a steady pace, otherwise people affected may start to get confused again. False starts can dilute the goodwill and slow the momentum. Opponents of the change only need to do nothing and it will die of a thousand cuts. It is important that the responsibility for progressing the plan is clearly assigned or delegated, and that, at each stage, it is ratcheted up so that it cannot slip back.

TIPS FOR MANAGING CHANGE

Here are some general, final tips on managing change through project management. These tips have been accumulated from a number of sources and from a general management background as well as from the field of change management:

- Communicate the change and about the change — generate as much discussion and debate about it as you can.

- Avoid surprises — keep people informed (in advance and throughout) and give lots of feedback.

- Pilot the change in a smaller area (where possible).

- Double your estimation of the amount of time you think it will take.

- Be prepared to change yourself.

- Reward the change.

- Make sure to have key stakeholders (both inside and outside the organisation) working actively for the change.

- The more uncertainty there is about how to change and which direction to take, the more you should involve stakeholders in the decision-making process.

- Look after your stamina — establish a sense of urgency and dynamism but keep enough energy for the implementation of the change.

- Don't be afraid to be visionary and to talk about the "big picture" — you can always move down to a smaller picture level if people have trouble with seeing the big picture but, if you start at the level of small picture detail, you might never be able to get away from talking details.

AND FINALLY . . .

You have come to the end of this book on managing change. Before we let you finish, though, there are just a few final thoughts on this process of which we want to remind you. The first of these concerns the notion of finishing itself — you have spent a few hours reading this book, a very small amount of time compared to the planning and implementation of any change. When we get to reaching the "final milestone" on anything, be it the reading of a book or the implementation of a major change, we like to feel that it is over, has ended, and has been properly closed. In management terms, this is often referred to as "signing off". It is an important psychological issue as none of likes to think of things which have loose ends left trailing.

In relation to the changes which you manage, you will always have to sign off officially at some stage so that you can move on to other things. Marking this signing off in some symbolic way will help you, and your change team, to psychologically move on from the current change to the next "chapter" in your working life. Often, for the change team, the best way of signing off on a change is to have a review session at the end (where you evaluate yourselves on your achievement of both the substantive objectives and relationship objectives — remember the chapter on negotiation?) and to have a really good night out at the end, a night where all the stresses and strains can be got out of the system, mulled over, laughed at, mourned even, and packed away (this is one occasion where you might *not* want to involve the clients!).

Speaking of the clients — those who commissioned the change or who are about to benefit from it — it is often necessary and desirable to leave them with some comfort zone at the end of the change project too. For clients, this can usually mean leaving some sort of support system to ensure the continued implementation and "bedding down" of the change in spite of the occasional hiccups and trouble spots which frequently occur in making any change part of the new normality. (Things are much more difficult to make "normal" when there is continued anxiety or nervousness about them.) This does not mean that you leave the door open for ever so that your commissioning clients can walk back in for your help should something go wrong — it simply means that, if something does go wrong after implementation and they cannot resolve the issue for themselves, they can have access to you for help for a limited period of time afterwards. If you are worried about this being an inordinate claim on your time, factor this support system into your budget for the change project. Make the price of the support sufficiently high so that the client will think before asking for it, but not so high as to deter the client from ever asking for it. After all, the idea of leaving a support system behind is to provide the client with some comfort but not to encourage him or her to become too complacent.

Good luck with whatever change projects you take on in the future — we hope this book will help to reduce some of the stress that you might possibly be feeling about managing these changes, and give you good guidelines for how to get the job done and get it done well.

Appendix

CALCULATION OF PROBABILITY IN ESTIMATES

A single-point estimate of the time required to complete any task can only be right or wrong — in other words, it only has a 50 per cent chance of being right.

Estimates within ranges (i.e. ranging from the most pessimistic to the most optimistic assessment of the time required) give a much truer picture and reflect the uncertainty that is inherent in managing change.

However, it may be difficult to get clients or senior managers to accept estimates with ranges. They generally want to know when exactly the change will be fully implemented and may be reluctant to accept an estimate such as "it might be finished in 15 months or it might be 23 months or anywhere in between, depending on the circumstances".

Programme Evaluation and Review Technique (PERT) is a commonly-used method in project management, especially when the projects are about the introduction of new, large or complex changes. PERT uses a relatively simple formula to calculate the probability of accuracy of estimates (and can be used for time estimates or budget estimates). This allows you to be fairly confident that your estimates will be accurate. However, to be this confident, some work is required and PERT-type calculations of probability can take up time (although, with the help of spreadsheets, this is not necessarily inordinate).

To calculate the probability of an estimate being right, you start by estimating the width of the range that is possible — a figure is picked for the most likely time needed (T_L), for the most pessimistic estimate of the time needed (T_p), and for the most optimistic estimate of the time needed (T_o) and this exercise is carried out *for each task*. The figures are then inserted into the following formula:

$$T_E = \frac{T_O + 4T_L + T_P}{6} \text{ (where } T_E \text{ is the expected duration)}$$

So, for example, if we were looking at the time required for the task "installation of office equipment" which might take anything from one month up to six months, depending on how quickly our supplier can source it from the US, we might have the following situation:

$$T_E \text{ (estimates given in weeks)} = \frac{4 + (4x8) + 24}{6}$$

which would give us an expected duration of 10 weeks.

Some people believe that estimates do not fall in a normal curve distribution and that the above formula is, therefore, going to give a overly-favourable expected duration. To correct for this over-favourability, the following formula is constructed of the same elements as the previous one but weighted differently:

$$T_E = \frac{T_O + 3T_L + 2T_P}{6} \text{ (where } T_E \text{ is the expected duration)}$$

If we use the same example as before and applied this formula to it, we would get a figure of 12.66 weeks as our expected duration.

The choice about which of these two formulae to use is yours and will probably be based on a number of factors which are as much political (what will your stakeholders accept?) and emotional (how much confidence do you have in your own capacity and in that of your team?) as rational.

Now that you have an expected duration for each task, you can go on to calculate the probability of your expected duration being accurate. This is done by calculating the standard deviation around each task's expected duration, using the following simple formula:

$$\text{Standard Deviation} = \frac{T_P - T_O}{6}$$

Again, going back to our example, this would give us a standard deviation of 3.33 weeks (a relatively large standard deviation because of the width of the range (4 to 24 weeks) for this one task). The reason we calculate the standard deviation is we can only be 50 per cent accurate using our expected duration of 12.66 weeks (we are using the more cautious of the two estimates because we have never used this supplier before) but:

- There is a 68.3 per cent probability that the task will be finished within one standard deviation (3.33 weeks) of this expected duration (i.e. between 9.33 weeks and 15.99 weeks).

- There is a 95.5 per cent probability that the task will be finished within two standard deviations (6.66 weeks) of this expected duration (i.e. between 6 and 19.32 weeks).

- There is a 99.7 per cent probability that the task will be finished within three standard deviations (9.99 weeks) of this expected duration (i.e. between 2.67 weeks and 22.65 weeks, although this is somewhat of a statistical fantasy as we have already said that the earliest possible completion time for this task is 4 weeks).

It might not seem as if the above exercise would add much more to "intelligence" about the change project than you already knew. However, going through this exercise for each task does enable you, as manager, to get an overall idea of how long the change is going to take and what sort of margins you are working within and, if you are pushed by your stakeholders, it always impresses them if you quote the exact probabilities! Statistics can "lie", of course, and you shouldn't be overawed by them. They won't make your change project come in on time, they can just make it seem that way (which is often very reassuring to those financing it.)

INDEX